Best Wish to Mayor l Hope yo... Jim Nelson 7-9-2010

DYING TO LIVE

The Life & Times of Jimmy Nelson

(an autobiography)

by

James W. Nelson

At the end is my latest short fiction

WAITING TO DIE

FOR A HUNDRED YEARS MANKIND HAS FEARED THE PANDEMIC,

AN EXTRAORDINARILY-MUTATED VIRUS, THAT VICIOUS CREATURE THAT CANNOT BE SEEN BY THE NAKED EYE.

Dedicated to my late parents,

Russell & Lois Nelson

They never gave up on me

INRODUCTION

(JIMMY NELSON IN A NUTSHELL)

Born October 18, 1944, Walcott, North Dakota, in a little farmhouse on the prairie. At 5 years old he met James R, his best friend for life; at 6 he received his first kiss—and on the lips—from Maxine (he'll never forget it); at 7 he saw his first love and discovered imagination; at 10 he survived a tornado, which destroyed the family farm and put his entire family in the hospital; at 12 his first fight (he lost; but, unbelievably, 30 years later, the other guy says *he* lost); at 14 he quit school (the social shock of leaving a one-room country schoolhouse for the town school was too much); at 15 his first job (doing chores for a farmer 7 days a week for $25.00, not /day but /week), also his first car (1948 Chevie 2-door; and, no, he doesn't still have it); at 17 he joined the US Navy (and talk about a social shock...); at 18 submarine duty and his first beer...same day his first drunk; at 19 his first, well, you know; at 20 he survived drowning; at 21 he met Sue in Sydney, Australia, his second love and the love of his life (unfortunately his sub left the harbor and he never went back); at 30 he started writing and met his third love; at 33 he lost that love; (during the next 13 years no first anythings but 3 failed businesses, a flower and gift shop, a greenhouse, and fence contractor, a period best forgotten); at 46 he got his first publishing (The Real Meaning of a Quarter in PKA's ADVOCATE...no payment); at 49 his first parachute jump; at 51 he lost his dear father; at 52 he lost his dear mother; also at 52 he met his fourth love and lost her to an aneurysm, at 55 he moved to the country and began building a home; at 65 he is publishing this book.... To fill in the lines and years, just experiencing, enjoying, anticipating and sometimes fearing, the endless palette of life.

I have been in love, and in debt, and in drink, this many and many a year. Alexander Brome 1620-1666

CONTENTS

DYING TO LIVE

(an autobiography)

THE LIFE & TIMES OF JIMMY NELSON

Prologue

BANG!

This terrible sound brings me out of sleep instantly, and ready, *half,* ready, to face whatever problem is there. The sound is my second-hand, newly-installed, hooked, door, sprung open and crashed against the side of the house. The only other time I have heard this sound was fifty-four years ago, just as a vicious tornado slammed the porch door open and roared into my family's lives. This time it's not a tornado but a ferocious straight November wind. (I would hear later, gusts to fifty mph.)

I'm fully clothed; I've just spent my first night, on the couch, in my new house. Four prefabricated walls and a roof nailed together: Sixteen by twenty-four feet bolted to the middle of a twenty-four by sixty-foot concrete slab. Not very finished. But I'm here, this is my home, and I will spend the next twenty-four hours protecting it. My belongings, in boxes, no longer covered by a tarp, piled on the concrete slab on the north side of the house, are, literally, blowing away.

But I am getting way, way, ahead of myself.

1

MANY BEGINNINGS

One of the darkest periods of my life came to a close sometime in April or May, 1999. I just wanted the pain to stop. It had and it hadn't. I can't honestly say what caused that disturbing episode that lasted for months. (Unfortunately, those feelings reminded me of the very darkest period of my life, which I'll expand on later, *much*, later.) I don't know. Some things had happened.

First my dear father died. Then one year later my dear mother. Then three months later my dear Julia died. (Julia's—and other names pertaining to Julia—have been changed. The events surrounding her are still too recent.) She was my best friend, my partner, my fiancé. We were talking about getting married. The word 'fiancé' had actually been breathed between us. Six-year-old Laura was in the back seat. Very likely she heard that word. But also very likely it disappeared from her play world just as quickly as it arrived. Had Julia and I used the words 'wedding' or 'marriage' maybe it would have stuck with Laura.

But what did it matter if Laura heard us right then anyway? Sooner or later we would include her. We would ask her permission, and to stand with us when it happened. And the word 'adoption' came up. I brought it up. I wanted to adopt Laura as soon as possible. I loved her. I wanted her to be my daughter. Then Julia died, and lay alone in her car for twenty-four hours before I found her.

She was cold and stiff and she was dead. And while I held her I watched my life fly before my eyes, and I knew, right then, that I would lose Laura too. Maybe because I made that unconscious prediction I caused our separation. I don't know. What I do know is that knowing Laura, having that six-year-old child in my life even for the short time she was there, changed my life forever.

All those losses—my father, my mother, Julia, Laura, and years earlier losing the farm—had torn at me a little differently. A little deeper. But blame them for that despair? Blame anything? I think not. Maybe I'm just weak sometimes. But how can I be weak? I had such a happy childhood. So good, in fact, that I sometimes feel guilty. Why should I have had a happy childhood when so many millions in the world don't?

Maybe writing these memoirs will help continue that journey from darkness. Julia's death was July 13, 1997. I spent the next two years living day-to-day, not in depression, exactly, but not happily, either. I'll finish Julia's and Laura's story later, too.

I guess I finally decided that a major change was in order. So in August, 1999, I hire an auctioneer and put my home and many belongings up for sale. This will be my third auction, and the happiest. The first two were farm auctions, not so happy, not happy at all, and they lead into a part of my life I'm not ready to expand on yet.

So, in October, 1999, myself and six friends put up those four walls and the roof in one day (just like an old-fashioned barn-raising), and about two weeks later, in November, I moved in and got that rude awakening by the wind.

But, like I said, this story comes later.

****

First I'll jump to the Navy. I was seventeen. I had quit high school two years earlier. And I had just had a minor disagreement with my dad. We never had major disagreements. That's right: We *never* had major disagreements. I feel kind of good about that. So, anyway, what was left?

Well, the Navy, of course.

So I go to the recruiter in Wahpeton, North Dakota. My plan is for the Marine Corps, not the Navy. I hadn't even yet considered the Navy. I wanted to be macho. (Although, at the time, I had never yet heard the word 'macho'.) The Marine recruiter's door is locked. He must have been on vacation that day. But I want to enlist. I want to get the hell off the farm and the hell out of North Dakota for awhile. I will eat those words a thousand times—nay, ten thousand times a thousand times. But memory of the farm, of someday getting to return to it, will sustain me.

Right across the hall from the Marine Corps recruiter is the Navy recruiter. His door is open and he's looking for recruits. I wonder. Do these guys get commissions?

I don't remember his name but I do remember his look. A little taller than me (I max out at 65½ inches [if I'm soaking wet]). Black crewcut (definitely in style in May of 1962). And a crisp dress blue uniform. I'll never forget him. I'll also never forgive him. No, just kidding. If I saw him today I would thank him. Not for keeping me out of the Marine Corps but for launching me on a great adventure.

I will never know how lucky I was not to join the Marines. More than likely I would have gone to Vietnam. Most likely I would have seen combat. And very, very, likely, I would have come home even more emotionally fucked up than I did. And sometimes still am.

Sorry, but the word 'fuck' is going to occasionally appear in these pages. It became part of my vocabulary because it fit so many places where just no other word seemed to express feelings properly. Fuck this and fuck that, ya fuckin' fucker. See what I mean? But I don't think I overuse the word. I also don't think I overused it even back then in the Navy, and I don't use it any more or less today, just when necessary.

(Or maybe things would have gone just the opposite. Maybe the Marine Corps would have turned me into an unshakable man. I will never know. Just one more of those hindsight things that people like to refer to when they wonder if some life decision was correct or not.)

Just a few days later I am saying goodbye to my family and my two best friends: Classmates for the first ten grades, James and Sarah. If I recall, they were graduating from high school that night.

My class and I'm not with them. I think I might have delivered to Sarah a graduation gift. I don't remember if I gave one to James. James and his brother Ronnie, and sisters Lianne and Mercedes, and their parents Oscar and Mabel, all became my early best friends. Many, many, happy hours I would spend at their home, while James taught me about hunting, fishing, trapping, and sold me my first gun, a lever-action MARLIN 39A. (No, I don't still have it, unfortunately.) And even though James taught me about hunting, etc., I never followed through and became much of an outdoorsman. But those experiences did produce those early childhood memories. James and I first met when we were about five years old. It's one of my first memories. But we were both "James" so we became James and Jimmy, and, later, James became Jesse James, but, to me, he'll always be James: James and Jimmy forever. More about James later, too.

Sarah was my other best friend in those early childhood days, and I spent many happy times playing with her and her five sisters and one brother. Her parents, Connie and Louise, were one of three sets of extra parents I had in that community.

Anyway, James accompanied my parents and me to Fargo where the Navy had paid for a hotel room. Wow. There I joined about a dozen other North Dakota boys. Yes, we were boys; two or three might have been 21 or more but for the most part we were snot-nosed kids who didn't have a clue. Oh yes, and I bought my first pack of cigarettes that night. OASIS. Menthol. They were long, filtered, and tasted funny. But I was as cool as everybody else. Before this I had often lifted my dad's straight CAMELS, and later, straight CAMELS—the Lord of all cigarettes—would become my cigarette of choice for the next twenty years.

The next morning things started getting uncool, and fast, and didn't let up for three months. First thing, physical. We had to get naked. "Bend over and spread'em." (Where the hell is my friendly recruiter?) The only thing I remember about that physical is some guy poking his finger in my ass. Did they use (even have?) latex gloves back then?

Then a written test. I don't remember any questions. One guy didn't pass. I remember his face. His name was Roger. And I remember another guy whose name was Duerr. On June 1, 1962, Duerr and I get to raise our right hand and get sworn in. Later he and I flunk a harder written test. We get dumped out of the company we had just spent the last four weeks with and get to—carrying every fucking thing the Navy had yet given us, including an M-1 rifle with no firing pin—struggle back over that bridge separating the regular Navy boot camp from Hell's Island.

I could have cried that day. Surprised I didn't.

(Where the fuck is my recruiter?)

I remember my dad at times like this. I have so many, many, good memories of him. And no bad ones. I remember especially my first memory with him. I was four or five. He was building a fence around the pond. Couldn't have the milk cows getting their udders wet, and sometimes muddy. And I was with him. What I remember is just being there, seeing him working while I watched. There was an aura around him. Sunshine, sunrays...how can I describe it? I worshipped him. I loved him.

I'm going to jump to my father's heart bypass now. You'll find that I may jump around quite a lot, but, when something comes up, I feel I should finish it.

2

ICU DIARY

We didn't know. We didn't understand back when Dad first began having chest discomfort, and what we did know we didn't take seriously. When the heart attack came it was severe, with much damage, and would require a triple bypass.

But when it actually came, it was, again, just chest discomfort, a tightness, no severe pain. But maybe my father just has a high threshold for pain. Maybe he can take more before admitting that it really hurts, more than other people, more than me.

****

The first night was difficult. I arrive home alone from St. Francis in Breckenridge, Minnesota, in daylight. Getting from the car and upstairs to bed takes a full hour, and darkness, so deep are my thoughts.

Worried about a future without my dad, whom I've rarely made proud and now could lose him, I was taking his heart attack less bravely than he. Self-doubt, self-pity for myself was plaguing me as much as worry for him. For I'm not really worried about him. If he goes to the next world now he will get the best there is, and will be happy there, released at last for whatever he's wanted to do for all these seventy-eight years.

He's bright now, after the diagnostic angiogram here at St. Luke's (now MERITCARE), in Fargo, North Dakota. The dye has gone into the arteries around his heart, created the x-rays, and now he's resting. Six hours he must lie flat on his back, not moving his right leg, immobilized with twenty pounds of bagged sand upon it, while the puncture from the catheter in the leg vein heals. Moans come from him—not from pain but from the discomfort of not being able to move his right ankle.

But he faces it.

Better than me as I repeat and repeat the long walk down the carpeted hall, hearing the squeak of my shoes, the beep of heart monitors, seeing cardiac nurses moving silently, swiftly from room to room. And back to room 277. My father is hooked to one of those monitors. How small he looks there in his bed, how frail, dependent. How I wish I could help him.

****

Suddenly six hours have passed. The nurse, a sprite of mercy, is magically here to remove the bag of sand, to help him lift his leg for the first time, to bend the knee, to massage and help ease the discomfort. The six hours are past. As he was told beforehand, the worst part of the angiogram would be those six hours.

And so it has been.

Then the news from the cardiologist, a kind man, soft-spoken yet brisk in his speech: Severe heart attack. Damage to the heart muscle. Much blockage. It will be decided later whether to try to control with drugs, or surgery. Surgery could be dangerous. He doesn't specify what that danger might be. His age? His rheumatoid arthritis? Probably a combination, but then it doesn't really matter what, for the real danger is the possibility of another heart attack.

More time passes. More long walks up and down the hall.

The surgeon arrives, also soft-spoken. His surgical skills emanate from him. I trust him immediately. He has reviewed the angiogram pictures and has conferred with the cardiologist. He recommends surgery. To remove a vein from the right leg, to open his chest, and to use the vein to bypass the blockages. About four of them.

The words reach my head like an electric shock. A tight spot forms in my own chest, my stomach…somewhere, and my eyes threaten to boil over. I see my father dying. I don't want to lose him. I love him.

But the facts are in. We should have taken them seriously, sooner. Now is but to make the decision. And wait. Only about a half a minute passes during the decision. Tomorrow. He will go up to the third floor at about six-thirty.

So soon? Saturday? How could this have happened? Not too long ago he was doing errands and chores for senior citizens older than himself, and mowing their lawns, four with his own. No matter the answers to those questions. About noon tomorrow we will learn how the operation went. Three to six hours on the table.

****

Back to the family room. It will be a long wait, but we will wait, each in our own way, our own thoughts. The others. I've been so insulated in my own thoughts that I have nearly forgotten them. My mother, a dear little white-haired lady who has never been without her man. My sister, Gerry, who only recently came through her own hip-replacement surgery. My other sister, Helen, overworked running her pizza parlor restaurant but coming from across the state, and will drive all night. And all the rest of the family not here. Nine grandchildren. Ten great-grandchildren.

So we wait with our chest-spasms, watery throats, boiling eyes, and whatever emotions the others might be feeling.

I look around at the other families with loved ones here at the intensive-care unit, second floor east. One woman, her mother and her aunt, we've made friends with; we've even shared some laughs, something about making a commercial—another family joins in. The things that go on in the family room.

Later the three are gone, no doubt with their loved one, who is waiting for a balloon insertion to her heart artery. An emergency team flies past the family room door, doctors, nurses, technicians, so many of them.

Everybody looks at everybody else. Faces are sober. Hearts throb. Eyes boil. Whose loved one is it? My mother steps to the hallway. I follow, and see the woman we've met holding one of two doors to the unit open. The emergency must have been theirs. Later I ask. "Yes, but she's OK again," she tells me, "They watch so closely here." The exact words I'm unsure of, but empathy passes between us. Two people, names unknown, waiting to hear of loved ones.

Everyone here is waiting for news. Some good. Some bad. Throughout the day friendly and warm hospital staff appear at the door to call a name. The hours go on. Names and faces change but the atmosphere remains the same. This rapport between and among families who have never met goes beyond friendly and warm to the deepest of compassion. For everyone is here for the same reason. Everybody knows.

And so we wait. Nineteen hours until tomorrow noon, June 13, 1987.

****

Eight p.m. The nurse from the third floor is in my father's room, telling all of us about the operation tomorrow. The tubes, catheters, electrodes to expect, where they will be attached and inserted. Every new procedure she explains and illustrates with charts and pictures drops my heart with a thud. It almost sounds like torture, but they are only the techniques of our expanding medical science knowledge, "...things we do every day."

Maybe so, but never before to my father.

Again I think of how small and frail he looks, and remember how tall and strong he has been so many times in the past. Other surgeries. Bouts with arthritis. The day we hauled—and he threw above his head into the barn to me—500 bales of heavy alfalfa hay. The time he lifted me—back then almost as big as he—pail, stool and all, from a trap between the wall and a bucking, kicking, milk cow.

I look at my father's chest, and imagine the red incision, the ribs spread, his heart and lungs beating in the open air. It's what happens up to three times a day here we're told. But, again, never to my father.

The nurse from the third floor talks and explains on. Dad is taking everything so bravely, but then he has always taken things bravely. I hope he doesn't sense the unbraveness in his son.

Were I in his place I'd be staring at the ceiling, not wanting visitors, not wanting to know about these 'procedures' or anything else, but just to get it over with.

Dad's comment, "Nothing's bothering me."

He doesn't know for a fact that he's going to get better; he has accepted that he might not get better, that he might not make it at all, but whatever happens he's ready for it. I thank God he's reached that acceptance. I don't know if I have or not, I only know—as I lean over and kiss his forehead—that I might not see him alive again.

Fifteen more hours.

****

Morning and back at the family room. Eight-thirty. Many faces are the same. New ones have arrived, including my sister, Helen, and another aunt to the woman we met yesterday.

The minutes tick by. My father is up there now getting his heart fixed. Every person who walks past the door causes us to look up. Is it the doctor? No.

Fifty minutes ago a staff person appeared at the door and told us it was over, that they were closing, that the doctor would be down in fifteen minutes, or so.

Fifteen minutes? But fifty have passed. So we wait.

****

It's over. The surgeon waves and smiles as he enters the family room. Arteries very small. One by the heart valve, where the damage was, might not do any good. But it went well, better than he expected.

We go to Dad's room with the doctor, all of us, including my brother-in-law, Don, who has just arrived. We look at Dad, lying flat and still, his chest rising and falling heavily as a machine breathes for him, tubes, catheters, wires, everywhere. He still looks small and frail, but I guess he's stronger than we knew.

****

More hours pass. He's awake, but with the breathing tube remaining he can't talk. So hard to see him like this. My dad. Swathed in tubes and bandages. He wants to talk to us so bad, but can't.

Still more hours pass. The breathing tube does not come out. But it's been twenty-four hours. The nurse, bright-eyed, warm, compassionate, tells us he has been tested with the machine off, and when he sleeps—which is off and on constantly—he stops breathing on his own. They will not remove the tube until they're sure, because re-inserting it is traumatic for the patient.

So the tube stays, maybe another twenty-four hours.

****

He wants to talk so bad, to communicate. He finally communicates to me: Paper, pen, clipboard…he writes, "Who died?"

"Nobody." The nurse (bless her and all the others) answers him immediately, "They just left, they got better." That satisfies him. He is in a co-ed ward with three other beds (other patients coming and going) with round-the-clock observation, one nurse to a patient. "In his still-anesthetized condition," the nurse tells us, "It's easy for him to see things in here and get wrong ideas."

Later more communication tries. He wants the clipboard left at his side. Again he's satisfied. He will write when it comes to him, what he wants to write, and when he can. We'll see.

He's sleeping when our pastor arrives. Pastor Jeff suggests we all hold hands as he says a prayer. Later Dad does communicate —though with scribbly writing—that he wants THE DAILY NEWS from Wahpeton, North Dakota, for the last five days. An avid reader, he must keep up with things.

****

June 15. He's off the respirator. First comment, "At least I can talk today." First question to me, "Have you picked strawberries yet?"

I tell him I haven't been home, and comment that the reason he was on the respirator so long was because when he slept he didn't breathe on his own.

"Ha, I was breathing on my own all the time."

"A real fighter," one of the nurses said of him.

I guess he is.

3

MANY BEGINNINGS (continued)

Returning to the further back past, that pond became a special place for me. Only about twenty feet across but I loved it there. The willows, a giant cottonwood (where I built a tree platform, not a house) the birds (once even a sandhill crane), the snakes and tadpoles and salamanders and snails, even the stinky aroma of that duckweed-covered water. I kept going there as an adult, to do nothing. Nothing but sit or stand and observe nature quietly, reverently.

My first memory of my mother is a little different, and a little more vague: I was maybe three or four, and I have heard this story so many times that I think I actually remember it. We were coming home from shopping and I wanted Mother to carry me. Well, she had her hands full and couldn't. So, I got mad and sat down, of all places on the railroad track. Mother must have known something I didn't because she went on without me. A moment or so later the train whistled. I don't know how far away it was, in the next county for all I knew, but that whistle made me move, and, as Mother has told it dozens, maybe hundreds of times, I ran all the way home.

It's not an unpleasant memory, though, because, since then, I've always enjoyed hearing a train whistle, but, of course, I've never sat on the tracks again. I pulled something similar with my sister, Gerry, who is five years older. Gerry is a fast walker. We had to walk a half mile to the country schoolhouse. She would get ahead of me and I would get mad and stop. So, with her golden patience for her little brother, she would either wait for me, or come back and get me. Boy, I must have been a brat in those days. My other sister, Helen, ten years older, I remember being the ring-bearer for her first wedding, and walking beside her new husband's very cute niece, Sharon, who was the flower girl, and who I don't remember seeing again.

But back to that first morning of my new career. Next we boarded a big plane. A turbo-jet. It had regular propellers but evidently was jet-powered too. I remember the stewardess. She was shorter. A little plump. Nice round ass. Gorgeous. The first woman I remember seeing away from North Dakota.

And away from home.

We flew first to Sioux Falls, South Dakota. On the way we hit (What? An air pocket?) Whatever. We hit it and we dropped, hard and fast, and left our stomachs on the ceiling. I don't think anybody puked. I remember that dear stewardess hurrying up and down the aisle making sure everybody was OK. What a woman.

At Sioux Falls we boarded a real jet. A big one. I don't remember if we made anymore stops. Maybe in Denver. I only remember the high points.

That's about forty-seven years ago, folks, and my memories of those three months of boot camp are foggy at best. I remember faces, but few names, and very few actual words of conversations. My next memory is landing in San Diego. Out the window it's pure white fog. Zero visibility. I remember the wheels hitting, a squeal, a major slowdown, and then that fog. I don't know how the pilot can see a thing.

I don't remember the stewardesses on the real jet. They must have been there because all jets have stewardesses, and in those days likely all were women. They must not have been memorable. I also didn't get to see any blonde bathing beauties when we landed in San Diego. In fact I wouldn't see another woman (except in the far, far, distance) for the next three months.

Maybe that's what makes the *somewhat* plump stewardess on the turbo-jet so memorable, because she was the first, and the last.

Somebody must be telling us what to do. When the plane stops we all stand, then we all follow the guy in front of us, out into that humid southern California dusk.

We're in the Navy now.

Then some black guy in a khaki uniform is yelling at us, "I want two lines and I will have two lines!"

Yes, we're in the Navy now.

We crowd onto a drab Navy gray bus. (In the next four years I'm going to get so fucking sick of Navy gray.) The black guy is still yelling at us. Not quite like the sergeant in FULL METAL JACKET, though. But yelling is yelling. The fear of God, or something, is being pumped into us. (Where the fuck is my friendly recruiter? Many times I will think of him, especially that nobody—*nobody*—is as nice and friendly as he was.)

Twenty-four hours ago I was still on the farm. Still with my mommy and daddy. Still with the milk cows, and the pigs, and the kitties, and my dog, and my pet rooster, Makoos. And I could still go out in the boxelder trees in the pig pasture for solitude, or to the pond for even deeper solitude. For the next four years and three months (especially the next three months) memories of the farm, of someday getting to return, will help sustain me.

Twenty-four hours later (I'm sure we went at least 48 hours from the time we got up in Fargo) we're still getting pushed around and yelled at. Nobody—*NOBODY!*—is nice and friendly. We get our sea bags, uniforms, ditty bags (shoe shine kit, toothbrush, soap, etc.) the book Uniform Code of Military Justice, serial numbers, billet numbers (Jesus, don't forget your billet number! [that's the number on the concrete grinder where you're supposed to stand]).

4

HELL'S ISLAND

We must have crossed the bridge to Hell's Island in the night. I don't remember the trip over, only that heartbreaking trip back with the boy called Duerr (to start all over again at day one) after we thought we had made it.

I don't remember too many details of those weeks in boot camp. I was too sleepy. Too scared. Too lonely. Too homesick. Many times I felt like crying, but I couldn't cry. For awhile I developed a propensity for nosebleeds. My company commander, who really wasn't a bad sort of guy, commented once that if I "...didn't stop having nosebleeds they might have to send me home...." (Home, my god, I'd love to go home!) I even, *considered*—once—forcing my nose to bleed, to at least not try stopping it—I wanted to go home!

We marched a lot, did calisthenics, did drills with our rifles, spit-shined our shoes, did laundry on concrete tables with scrub brushes and a little soap, hung our clothes on clotheslines without clothespins, pressed our dungarees, etc., with our hands, and stood plenty of inspections.

Somehow I failed only three personnel inspections during my whole career. I'll touch more on them as they come up. Oh yes, and we spent plenty of time in classrooms learning about the United

States Navy. Especially the new terminology: A floor is now a deck; ceiling, overhead; wall, bulkhead; bathroom, head; rifle, piece; and a rope (and a whole host of other things) is a line, etc., etc. I still use many of those terms today, especially if I'm in a situation where I likely won't get questioned about what the hell I'm talking about.

For the first three weeks I excel in the weekly written tests. Then we get to pack up and march over that bridge to where the regular Navy boot camp is, where things are rumored to be easier. (Things are not easier. I suspect Hell's Island existed for the simple reason of transition, a feeling of moving onward.) Because that bridge would most certainly bring a feeling of moving backward.

The fourth week brought failure of the 3-5 day test.

Now I have to go back across that concrete bridge and start all over again at day one. How could this have happened?

But I won't be going alone.

Duerr is coming with me.

We load up everything: Fully packed sea bag. Blankets and pillow. Piece. Ditty bag. It's more than I can carry at once. I just know it!

Looking back at that day I have to wonder...did the Navy somehow realize what a depressing, frustrating, ego-rending journey that would be? Is that why Duerr and I were allowed to go not accompanied by some chief or upperclassman who would yell at us? Did the Navy know we (at least I) would be close to tears? Did the Navy have a heart? Even there and then?

It was hot. It was long. It was a struggle. Duerr and I help each other, and we do make it. But upon arrival we're split into separate companies. I never see Duerr again. I think the name is somewhere around the Hankinson/Lidgerwood/Wyndmere, North Dakota area but I've never attempted to find him.

I wonder if he has memories even nearly the same.

So I'm alone again. I know no one.

5

COMPANY 311

You remember I said my first company commander wasn't a 'bad sort of guy'? Well, he wasn't. I also don't remember his name. Chief Thomas was my next company commander. (*Choker* Chief Thomas, I would later learn at Class A school, from Instructor First Class Petty Officer Raspberry E-6.) Thomas was black. He joined the Marine Corps when he was sixteen. He made two World War II landings in the Pacific before he was discovered to be too young. But they didn't kick him out. They then let him join the Navy where he worked his way to E-12, the top of the enlisted men's ranks. Yes, he was tough. And we—me and seventy-nine other snot-nosed kids like me—were going to make Company 311 not only his last boot camp company before his retirement, but also his *BEST.*

He guaranteed it.

We would take all honors or we would bleed.

His first words to me, his reject from Company 309, "I'm going to watch you, Whitey."

At that time I didn't know black men sometimes referred to white men as "Whitey." I thought he was referring to my very bleached-blonde hair. Maybe he was. Another thing I will never know the answer to.

Anyway, I will never forget him.

And though he scared me, I liked him.

****

So for the next three weeks, again, we march and drill and go to class on Hell's Island. Again the rumor spreads that we'll have it easier when we go back across that bridge to where the regular Navy boot camp resides. Sorry, guys. I've already been there. It just ain't no easier. But of course I don't try to tell anyone this.

I don't remember the march back over that bridge.

Been there. Done that.

Now, along with the regular drills we begin some advanced training. We get to go into an enclosed space on a mock-up ship. We all have gas masks. Then they release the tear gas. Then we have to remember our classroom training and put the masks on. Correctly. But my mask fills with tear gas long before I get it on.

Another day they start a fire somewhere on that mock ship and we have to go in with fire hoses. And everybody gets to—at least for a few seconds—stand at the head of the line and open and close that valve with the tons of water pressure.

And we get firearms training with M-1s. I'm so damned afraid I'm going to get my thumb caught when I shove that 8-round clip into the firing chamber and release the cocking mechanism. In the movie THE LONGEST DAY, the late ROBERT RYAN does it so beautifully. I don't catch my thumb. And somehow I qualify as marksman. I feel macho that day, but I still have never heard that word.

I'm in the Navy now.

Oh, yes, and the swimming classes. Everybody doesn't have to go to swimming classes after the first lesson. And that first swimming lesson mainly is to determine who can swim and who can't. They have a unique way of determining that. We have to jump into the deep end and swim to the shallow end. And those who just sink cannot, evidently, swim. I, of course, sink. We've been told that if we can't swim they'll extend what I remember as a bamboo fishing pole to us and pull us out, but only if we just grab it and hang on, and not reach hand over hand in our haste to get out. "If you do that we'll just drop the pole and let you have it." And of course we'll just sink away again. And a couple dumbasses *do* do that. And of course they're given the pole and they just sink away again. But of course nobody is allowed to drown, just to think they're going to. I jump in. I sink. Instinct brings me thrashing to the surface. The pole is there. I grab it and hang on. I don't go hand over hand. They pull me in.

But now, on top of every other fucking thing we have to get done in one day, nonswimmers have to go to extra swimming classes. At a different time and place I would have been appreciative to learn to swim. Right now I can't exactly see it. After all, most of us are only heading to the ocean, where only the deepest mutherfucking water in the world is.

So we learn to float, back stroke, side stroke, and dog paddle while removing our dungaree bottoms, tying knots in the legs, then whipping them over our heads (which captures air) and laying forward on them and using them as temporary life preservers.

To graduate from swimming (everybody had to do it) we have to climb to a twenty-foot tower, stand at attention and step off (of course remaining at attention) and fall into the deep end. I'm so scared I could shit! The guy ahead of me goes. In another second or two I go. (Oh, yes, and "Don't look down" [looking down will cause your body to lean forward, you will hit on your stomach and you might pass out.]) Well, I do look down, all the way. I do a total belly flop. But I'm too damned scared to pass out. Adrenalin is so high I don't even feel any pain. I back stroke to the other end and climb out. Congratulations. You are now a swimmer. Yeah, right.

Our marching is beginning to shine. We're in cadence. Every left foot slams the grinder at the same time. Our guide-on bearers snap those flags smartly. I'm beginning to love marching. It's easy. It's macho. My feet do the work and my mind is allowed to go anywhere it wants. And, occasionally, in the far, far, far, distance, we see in the bright California sunshine somebody walking in colorful clothes. It's got to be a civilian. Sometimes it's wearing a skirt, with legs extending—It's a woman!

While marching, and any other time while in ranks, our eyes are supposed to be just one place: Planted on the back of the head of the guy in front of you. An air of something goes through the ranks. It's not a sound. Nobody would dare make a sound. It's more like an awareness, a feeling, a powerful intensity. But something about is different. I barely divert my eyes left. In the distance, about a block away, something is yellow—a dress! I see a shining mane of long blonde hair, and legs! Yes, a woman! No, a girl! She's young, in her teens or twenties—our age! Against the might of the United States Navy my head turns. I stare long and hard. We could as well have been given the order, "Company! Eyyyyyes LEFT!" because I am as sure as being alive that 160 eyes were fixed on that young woman in the distance.

Could she feel it? Did she have even a clue of how she affected us? Was she some company commander's daughter and she was here just visiting her daddy? (Her daddy who would have beat the hell out of all eighty of us for the dirty thoughts we were having about his little girl?) What the hell was she doing there? Maybe she was some hussy from the street, paid by the Navy just to be there and walk within a block of the marching companies, just to keep us horny fuckers reminded of what waited for us once we finished boot camp.

Some of us.

At seventeen I yet had not experienced sex of any kind. (And just one wet dream during that whole three months in boot camp!) But not even a kiss or a hug at home, except from family members. I've been in love many times though. Let's see, there were Sarah and Jeanette and Carol in my own class. And Judy and Cheryl and Marilyn in the next class younger, and of course Linda. (I fell in love with Linda when she was a tiny first-grader and I was a great big second-grader.) And Patsy, although I didn't fall in love with Patsy. In fact, there were times I wasn't even very nice to Patsy, and I'm sorry about that. I wasn't, *exactly,* mean to her, I just wasn't nice. And Patsy was damn good-looking, too. I'm sorry, Patsy, I hope you are doing well in life.

A few years later than first grade (I was maybe a freshman or an eighth-grader) we were at some school function in the gym at night. The lights were out except for the stage, and for some reason known only to God I was sitting next to Linda. James was on my other side and Gary (another classmate, but only for two years) was on Linda's other side. I'm sure this next action has been premeditated: These two boys start pushing Linda and me together. Of course we fight back (Why on earth did I fight that?) and a few times our heads bang together. Well, if I had any doubts about Linda, that head-banging settled it. I was in love with her and I always would be. Linda and I did dance a couple of slow dances in high school; I think she maybe even skated with me a couple times. But I will always remember those dances. Thank you, Linda. I wonder where you are today.

But, you know how it is. I'm in love with somebody, and that somebody is in love with somebody else, and that somebody is in love with still somebody else, and on and on and on. That's how it is, and that's how it'll always be.

Then there were the upper classes. Maxine, one year older. She gave me my first "romantic" kiss. We were about five and six years old (She was the "older" woman in my life.) I was at her house on her dad's farm after school. Their hired man, Alfred, somehow coaxed us into kissing, and on the lips. I didn't exactly fall in love with Maxine because of that but she did become a very special person in my mind. My next kiss would not arrive until I was well past eighteen. And that one was not romantic; I have to say it was… good—but strictly sexual. My first romantic kiss—after Maxine—didn't come until Sydney, Australia, and I was past twenty-one. But that's a later story too.

A couple years later Maxine and I are on opposite teams playing anti-I-over-the-barn at our one-room country schoolhouse. One team throws a ball over the building to the other team on the other side. When one team catches the ball they must run around to the other side and touch as many of the other team's players as possible with the ball, until none are left. On one of these team charges Maxine and I collide head on, and her head takes a chip out of one of my bottom front teeth. Since then I've had offers to "fix" that tooth (what with modern technology) but, no way. That's a love wound.

People in my own grade, like James (my best friend) Donald, Gary and Maynard, are peers, but kids older than me, in the next grades up, I think of a little differently. There was Larry and Richard and another Gary and Herbert and Timmy and Howard and Cecil and Reggie and Chucky and Orville and Wayne, and Shirley and Carrie, and, of course, Maxine. I guess they were role models, although back then nobody had heard of that terminology. So what then? Heroes? To a point, yes. Mainly I noticed how they treated other kids. If they were nice I felt good, if they weren't I felt bad. But no matter what, they were role models. What these older kids did, or didn't do, left an impression on me.

And there were others who caused me love in my heart. Some younger, some older, like Marilyn and Diane, my sister's classmates. Some from other schools who we played basketball against, and most names I didn't know but it seemed in every town there was at least one girl I at least "liked." But always from a distance. It was easy to like someone long as you never had to tell them. So I never learned how.

Basketball I loved. I really wanted to be a basketball hero, but I never learned how to dribble that damned ball! I got to play twice. Once in the B-squad: I made one field goal and one free-throw. And once in the A-squad, for about thirty seconds. The ball got passed to me (Who the fuck threw that ball to me?!) and I got rid of it quick! I didn't dribble, probably traveled, and passed it to Orville as quick as I could, and then Coach Mahoney got me the hell off the floor. Thanks, coach.

To get back to my growing love of marching, I felt relaxed marching, more responsive to things happening around me, and I think others felt that way too. Because some neat things happened. I even remember some comments, word for word (when someone actually dared to speak) so I can honestly repeat them here. You remember the new terminology we had to learn, well, some of us learned at different speeds. One guy got the new term for restroom (head) turned around when he once called out "When do we get to go to the rear?" I don't remember his face or his name, just his Texas drawl.

Our RCPO (Recruit Chief Petty Officer), the next in command when Commander "Choker" Thomas wasn't around, was big. I mean he was big. His name was Mahan. His face was sculpted something like KIRK DOUGLAS. I don't think I was afraid of him, exactly, but when he told me to do something, I did it. Our Master-at-Arms was a big scary guy, too. When two companies would meet at an intersection one would have to halt and wait. What determined who would halt I don't know. Maybe the rules were the same as two cars: the driver to your right has the right-of-way. Anyway Mahan was in charge that day and halted Company 311. The Company Commander from the other company barely broke stride as he swung close to Mahan and said, "You're big enough to eat hay and shit in the street!"

But of course everything that happened while marching was not so neat. We've been told, if the guy ahead is out of step, "Step on his heels!" I'm in step. I know I'm in step because I know the heavy beat of the drums is when my left foot is supposed to slam the grinder. And the guy ahead of me is in step. WE'RE ALL IN STEP! But the son-of-a-bitch behind me begins to step on my heels! I don't remember what I said to him. We're not supposed to talk in ranks. Anytime. But he soon stopped stepping on my heels. Now, forty-seven years later, I suddenly wonder…was somebody else stepping on *his* heels…? Hmmmm….You know, I don't think so. He was shorter than me and likely was the last one in the squad.

That incident, *then*, was the first of two times when I felt honestly violent toward a shipmate. I wanted to hurt him. I wanted to hurt him bad. It was one of those personal historic events that stay with you in Cinematic living color for life.

Sometime later he got caught smoking—along with another guy—where it was against the rules. They both got to sit inside an overturned garbage can and smoke to their hearts' delight. No, I didn't cheer. I didn't even feel like cheering. I also felt no compassion for him, but for the other guy, yes. Mostly I thanked God it wasn't me who got caught, though I don't remember thanking

God.

There were other times I felt compassion for guys who fucked up and got punished. I'll describe the worst I saw. Picture doing sit-ups. Not so bad, right? Now picture a picnic bench with a table not much wider than the seat. Now picture yourself sitting on the table part and hooking your feet under the seat, and leaning back till your head touches the other seat, and then doing a sit-up.

Still not so bad, right? If a guy is in any shape at all he probably can do that. And guys who fucked up got to do that. (I'm very sure I couldn't do it and I never—thank God—had to try.) But I'm still not done describing. If you really fucked up you had to hold your piece behind your head during these sit-ups. And if you really, really, fucked up you got to tie two pieces together and then do sit-ups. (You maybe remember, a piece is a rifle, and they weren't light.)

The guys who did sit-ups on picnic benches with two pieces behind their head went to the hospital and usually got sent back to another company. If they survived they got to stay, and usually they probably quit fucking up.

Company 311 was going to be Commander Thomas' best.

One way or another.

Fuckups in the company would not be allowed.

****

I only got punished once. And that time wasn't initiated by my company commander. We go to church every Sunday. Staying awake in church is a struggle. We go to bed at nine, but, rain or shine, we have to be up at four. There is so much to do—shit, shave, shower, get dressed, leave a spanking tight bunk, all uniforms folded, locker stored correctly and locked, laundry, shoes spit-shined, leggings tight around your shins...I could go on and on. What I'm saying is, we had a lot to do in a day, and we worked all day, and we had to get up early to get all that done. So, yes, it was a struggle staying awake in church. Another of those forever life event pictures in my mind.

The church is—sort of—like an amphitheater. Imagine a sea of tightly-shaved heads: Bobbing: Sleepy Navy recruits trying to stay awake. We are told, if the guy ahead of you starts bobbing his head "Slap'im with your white hat!" Yes, my head got slapped several times. No, I never felt violent toward the guy who slapped me. And no, I never had to slap the guy ahead of me. And that was good. I don't think I could have performed even that one simple act of violence without actually *feeling* violent. What the hell was I doing in the military?

Getting back to my story, going to church we marched together as a company. Returning to the barracks was different. With thousands of recruits leaving that church there is just no way of getting them all to line up with their correct company. Well, they could have, but to do it quickly would have been nearly impossible. So, we lined up with strangers, but still in companies of eighty men. Then we had to march to a grinder that was still quite a distance from our own barracks (and in the opposite direction!) halt, left or right turn, fall out, and then double time it to the barracks. Unfortunately, coming from church, we had to pass right by my own barracks.

And every Sunday I watch as other recruits leap out of formation and sneak back to their barracks. I mean, why go all that extra distance in the wrong direction? Every Sunday I watch others do it (and never get caught!) but, naive dumbass that I am, I never do. Except this one time. Everybody (well, not everybody) is doing it, so...

So I do too....

Well, this time there is a company commander watching.

And he starts yelling, "Stop! Halt in place!"

Well, almost nobody stopped. It was so easy to disappear into that disorganized dribble of blue and white uniforms, but, being the naive dumbass that I am, I stop.

In place. At attention.

And two others do.

Dumbasses all.

Whether those who did not stop ever got caught and punished

even worse than we did, I will never know.

The first company commander is joined by a second, then a third. Us dumbasses that stopped are then marched (and yelled at all the way) to an even more distant grinder where we get to double time around and around till we are exhausted, then we get to do calisthenics, then more double time, until we are all sorry, *really, sorry.*

But getting released from all that extra duty doesn't end it. The next morning we have to report to battalion headquarters for even more extra calisthenics, and then clean up duty of walking over and over that huge grinder picking up cigarette butts and any other foreign objects. I will never see a parking lot so clean as that viciously hot grinder.

But the very worst punishment of all is getting to explain to Company Commander "Choker" Thomas...why it happened.... He didn't punish me further; I don't know why.

Very soon after that I fail my first personnel inspection. A barely visible yellow ring on the sweatband of my whitehat. (At least I thought it was barely visible.) Commander Thomas caught me halfway to the second deck of the barracks. He jerks my white hat from under my belt (where we are supposed to put it right after entering any building: jerk it off, turn it inside out, fold it, and shove it under your belt). He looks at it, then slaps me across the face with it. I don't remember what he said but he used that term 'Whitey' again, and I'm sure he said something about not 'fucking' up again.

Well, by now I want to be part of Company Commander Thomas' last and very best boot camp company. I don't fuck up again. Nothing major anyway.

Then there is my second personnel inspection failure. This one is a locker and uniform inspection. Since I had already been to Hell's Island I already had my dress blues. Why the dress blues arrived at a different time than the rest of my uniform is another one of those things I will never know. Anyway, I already had my dress blues when nobody else in Company 311 did. And the dress blues are folded wrong. Thomas looks at me. I am mortified. I can still see his eyes. But for some reason that only Commander Thomas (and God) knows, he didn't punish me.

I get to stay in Commander Thomas' Company 311 and we graduate with top honors: Four gold stars on that flag.

We get a picnic for each of those gold stars, on base, of course, but still a respite from the daily grind. And, near the end we are allowed our first liberty...with the warning: "I don't care if you're over twenty-one! RECRUITS DON'T CONSUME ALCOHOL!" Well, I had yet tasted no alcohol in my very sheltered life anyway. Maybe a drop or two of wine at communion, but maybe my church had already gone to grape juice (I wouldn't have known which it was anyway.) So consuming alcohol is not on my mind. I just wanted to get away from boot camp for a few hours.

And I already had plans anyway. My parents had contacted a friend of theirs (Clint) in San Diego, a man I had never seen before. He would meet me at the gate and pick me out of a group of about a dozen marching raw recruits who all look the same. Sunburned, bald, in white uniform, "Jimmy, is that you?" He recognizes me because I look so much like my dad. He would take me to his home, then a fancy restaurant, finally to Disneyland. This friend of my father's would also take me, later, after I got to Class A School, to Tijuana, Mexico. But that's another later story.

I didn't make any close friends at boot camp. About the closest was Austin, a young black boy from Texas. On one of our liberties I ask him if he wants to go to Balboa Park Zoo with me. He doesn't want to and doesn't give me a reason. But I've always wondered, why? About the only reason I've ever come up with is, in the early sixties black people and white people hadn't yet begun to mix very well. We did fine in boot camp. We didn't dare do anything different. But to go on liberty together evidently was a different matter. Maybe he didn't dare be seen with a white man, or maybe he was afraid for me to be seen with a black man. Whatever. Austin, I didn't forget ya, bud. You're one of the very few names and faces I remember from boot camp.

6

TORNADO

Before I go on with my naval career I will touch on one of the other most important things that ever happened to me. You remember that loud bang! the very first word in my story, well, you're soon going to hear it again, only it's louder…and it tends to be terrifying. It was July 2, 1955. I was ten. Cool that morning but the afternoon turned sweltering. My nephew, Curtis, five, my very best friend at that time and who I considered almost my brother, and I, had been cleaning out the south side of the tar paper-covered garage. The plan is to set up a table or two for our farms and toy soldiers. It was a good plan.

By five-thirty we had finished sweeping the dirt floor. Mother calls supper. We head in. Huge thunderheads are rising over tall spruce trees in the southwest yard. Rain sprinkles. Sunrays make brittle contrast against the white house and dark clouds. Nothing about the changing weather seems really serious but we hurry faster anyway. We'll be safe inside.

But my dog, Pal, very small, somewhat Collie-like, stops, whines softly, then turns and lopes in the opposite direction, toward her refuge under the hoghouse, where she has raised several litters, and, as a puppy herself, hid on the day of her arrival to the farm.

But it has rained before and Pal has not gone to the hoghouse. (Did she already detect the changing barometric pressure? Or was it the sixth sense that some animals, and some people, have?) To Curtis and me, nothing seems serious. Nothing at all.

We slip through the east porch door and are greeted by the squeal of 13-month-old Celi, my niece and a jabbering bundle of smiles. She sees us and, propelling herself with crossed legs and feet, comes scooting over the floor on her bottom.

From the corner of the porch floor, with crayons and paper, three-year-old Becky, another niece, a beautiful and intelligent child with reddish-brown hair and bright blue eyes, asks my mother, Lois, "I'm so hot, Grandma, can I take my dress off?" Without waiting for an answer she snatches the hemline and peels it over her head. She does look more refreshed in just panties, so Curtis and I remove our shirts.

Later, all of us, including my dad, Russell, and sister, Gerry, 16, sit to eat. A special affair tonight for Mother has just returned from a Ladies' aid bake sale.

Supper is mostly finished by twenty to seven. Anxious to console Pal, probably still cowering under the hoghouse, and also to move my toys into the garage, I am first to leave the table. But upon reaching the porch I see a yellow glow outside. Unexplainable dread stops me.

The barn is about thirty feet high and sixty feet long. Beyond its peaked roof the sky is pale blue. The barn is bright red against the blue; its silver cupola is gleaming. The yellow glow fades. Outside begins to darken, fast, yet the sky beyond the barn remains friendly-looking mid-summer blue. Fears stabs at me as I hurry back to the kitchen.

Everybody is already up, standing silently at the double kitchen windows facing north, toward where darkness is spreading, covering the farthest treetops quickly, as if a sky monster is swallowing the sun. It is so quiet. Nobody is talking, and outside not even the sound of a bird. Nothing. The quiet is so intense it's becoming a pressure beginning to hurt my ears.

A roar is becoming apparent from the west, like a distant freight train, usually a pleasant sound but now insidious, rumbling, approaching nearer and nearer, faster.

From where there is no railroad.

"Boy, we're going to get an awful hailstorm," Mother announces, "Hear that roar?"

"I think so too," Dad agrees.

But it's more than a roar. It's a sound I've never heard, nor imagined, and it's beginning to terrify me.

It's terrifying all of us. We keep staring at the silence and calm right outside, at the green of our farmyard, at the blue sky where ragged fingers of black cloud are finally edging into view, looming over our thought secure, tree-surrounded farmstead.

From the floor, Celi, sensing terror from the rest of us, begins to whimper. Gerry immediately kneels and gathers the usually happy baby into her arms.

"What's a hailstorm, Grandpa?" Curtis asks.

BANG!

The crash is the east porch door, flung open. But there is no wind. Outside is still absolute silence, stillness except for the intensifying roar. Everybody gapes. Nobody knows what to do. Time is passing too quickly to be able to do anything. Dad heads for the porch door. Everybody watches him. Eyes wide, Curtis follows, "Grandpa, look at your car!"

We press against the kitchen windows. Outside the house yard fence the car is bouncing up and down. But it's so calm outside.

We couldn't know that fluctuating pressure preceding the storm is making strange things happen seemingly without substance. Dad didn't know. Mother didn't. Much too early in the century. The media blitz has not yet hit, consumer weather forecasting is still in infancy. Our communications is a radio not listened to during meals, a hand-powered telephone not ringing.

But nobody in the community yet knew either, for the storm had first formed several miles west in uninhabited pasture, then the tornado that came from it had hopped and skipped causing little damage, to escalate a mile west of our farm. There would be no warning. No time to get to the cellar. One entrance outside, another under linoleum in the kitchen. And still we have no realization we even need better shelter.

Like a balloon filled, the pressurized car pushes its weakest point, a poorly latched door, and pops it open.

"Mother, you didn't get the car door shut," Dad exclaims, "Now it'll blow open and break!"

Dad does not leave the house to close the car door, for the unknown fear grips us all, but he does step out slightly, grips the porch door, pulls it shut.

BANG!

It explodes right open again, harder, seeming to shake the house. The roar now seems right on top of us. The trees north and west of the barn begin straining, leaning east as if a mighty magnet pulls them, yet the house itself still feels no wind. Little Becky stands among us, as in nonthinking awe we watch the trees bending so far as to touch the ground.

Then the barn and other outlying buildings begin leaning east, again as if a magnet pulling, not wind pushing. Everything close is still so quiet. Farther away everything is happening so fast, and it's so hard to believe, and accept. We still have no full realization of a dangerous wind. No realization we should do anything but stand, watch, in shock believing that nothing so bad as what's happening could really be happening.

Suddenly the unseen magnet is winning. Everything beyond the house yard gate begins breaking apart, sending boards, shingles, branches flying around and around. The terrible roar now sounds like ten freight trains about to crash into the house. The pressure in my ears feels like I'm going under water.

The car door blows open, then wrenches and twists itself around to the front windshield, then it's moving on its own across the yard. The 60-foot windmill, like a matchstick, topples east. The barn and granary roofs lift, and are gone, disappeared. The barn, like a stand of dominoes, collapses to the east, its siding and insides erupting like a hail of arrows. Like a cardboard box, the wooden granary rolls across the yard, west, opposite everything else.

An animal, small and dark, hurries across the yard, toward the disintegrating barn, looking for a place to hide. Pal! I know it's Pal! But my mind cannot concentrate, cannot conceive anything but recognition of my beloved pet. The image of her, small and frightened, ingrains in my mind.

Pal disappears as dirt and other flying objects fill the air. Mindlessly I run for her. Dad grabs me, returns me to where everyone has moved away from the window. We're now clustered in the center of the room. And still we continue witnessing, dumb-like, the unimaginable disaster occurring outside.

Suddenly the house is shaking, furiously. Dishes are falling from cupboards, clattering, crashing, breaking.

"Everybody into the west bedroom!" Dad shouts, then begins guiding us there. But I glance back. The east porch is breaking away from the house. Wide-eyed Curtis is still there, engraining more memory, then disappears into a curtain of dust and debris.

The rest of us crowd into the small bedroom, *my* bedroom, where I've slept in safety all my life, awakening happily to birthdays and tooth fairy visits. I look back once more. The kitchen linoleum has bubbled halfway to the ceiling. The refrigerator is rocking back and forth as if dancing, crazily. Everything, everywhere, is moving, falling, breaking.

The horrible sound outside is like a brutal sandblaster crunching the walls. The only other real sound is Celi in Gerry's arms, crying, not in paralyzed shock like the rest of us.

Everything outside the west window is white, all white. The house groans, cracks, moving and twisting beneath our feet.

"Here goes the house." Dad says it calmly, resigned, for there is nothing he can do to stop it, nothing he could have done. No time. No warning. No prior experience.

The house is actually lifting into the air, doing the impossible...and breaking apart. The west window shrieks as it bursts from its casing, smashes into my back, ending my awareness for I don't know how long.

****

The next thing I remember is continuous thunder and lightening. Rain and hail is pouring in cold, terrifyingly-cold, torrents driven by fierce straight wind...and my screaming voice, "God, I don't want to die!"

From the night-like darkness, sitting though with her back broken, comes my mother's voice, "Jimmy, you're not going to die."

Dad struggles from the ground, pulls me up to sit, then stands, stares at an incinerated landscape, "Everything is gone."

Not a hole remains where several huge boxelder trees stood south of the house. The now fenceless lawn is bare dirt, scorched, as if a fire has swept by. The few remaining trees on the outskirts of where the thick grove had been are stripped of bark, have a burned appearance. No sign of buildings. Nothing. Only smashed and slivered boards.

The sound of galloping hooves comes from the north. The two black draft horses, Dixie and Daisy, are followed by ten wild-eyed, panting milk cows, running not as fast but bucking, kicking, their flopping udders swelled, unmilked, then are gone, disappearing into the gauze of shock surrounding us.

From beneath a section of wall comes Gerry's cry for help. Though his arm is cracked, Dad lifts it off as if cardboard. Then, strength gone, he sinks to the ground. No grandchildren in sight. Nobody with the strength or even presence of mind to search for them.

"I'll go get help," Gerry says, now sitting up.

"You can't," Dad answers, "Where would you go?"

Still crying I ask, "Daddy, are we in a dream?"

"No, Son. This is really happening."

So we lay in the cold and rubble of our farm with unknown

injuries and dirt ground into our skin, thinking—if thinking at all—that everybody would be like us, helpless, that there would be no help.

Headlights appear on the road. Always heavy foliage growth had prevented seeing lights except in winter, but now the grove does not exist. We watch the headlights until they stop right in front of us.

"Where are the children?" They ask.

Nobody knows. Three men have arrived. Art Blair, Dad's cousin, and his visiting sons, Woody and Johnny. They live one mile north, have watched the tornado destroy the farm, and came as soon as it was possible.

They load us. Becky and Celi, covered with dirt, are found almost immediately because the car had barely missed them. But no Curtis. Two men will stay to look. Curtis can't be seen because of day-darkness and because he is so covered with dirt, but within two hundred feet a frightened little boy is buried in sand to his waist, arm broken in three places, shouting and frantically waving his good arm.

Little talk occurs as we ride up to 100mph toward the nearest hospital at Breckenridge, Minnesota. I sit in front between Woody and Dad, who announces, "I'm freezing to death."

Mother and Gerry ride in back with baby Celi between them. Becky lies face down on the floor. Mother, unable to move herself, asks Gerry to move Becky off her face.

"No, I can't." Gerry holds her neck and head, unaware her neck is broken, "It hurts too bad."

Neither knows Becky's head is nearly crushed in several places, worst in back, and that lying on her back might have killed her.

Between them little Celi moves once, takes one breath.

"Little Celi is gone." Mother speaks with no emotion. There are no tears from anyone.

Six miles from the hospital a rear tire blows out. Passers-by have it changed in minutes. While there a woman announces that bad weather is coming.

"Oh, no!" Gerry cries out, "We can't go through it again!"

Minor damage did occur in the Breckenridge, Minnesota/Wahpeton, North Dakota area. Whether the same storm cell is unknown.

At the hospital the undertaker pronounces both granddaughters dead and asks Woody to take them to the funeral home.

"No, I can't. There's a little boy back there who hasn't been found, and I'm going back to look for him!" In fact, Curtis had been found and already was at the hospital.

The undertaker, Joseph Vertin, then picks Becky up. When he turns her over in his arms she moans, prompting him to carry her four flights to the emergency room.

Our wounds are attended by Doctor N.R. Kippen, a kind man who continued to attend my parents until they died in 1996 and 1997. Later I hear that wire brushes were used to clean our sand-pitted skin, especially Curtis' and mine, as we had been without shirts. I remember pain, hearing myself and Curtis screaming, but nothing more during those early hospital hours.

My other sister, Helen, has arrived. A young girl stays by her side throughout that first night. Helen later describes her as a guardian angel, and does not see her again.

Dad is seen by Helen first. His face appears as if a hot iron has rubbed across it. "Helen, we couldn't find Curtis."

Mother, lying on her stomach while her deeply gashed hips are worked on, is next. "Helen, your baby is dead."

Turning to leave, Helen walks past Gerry, who is cut so badly Helen doesn't recognize her. Gerry sobs helplessly that she had been holding Celi and lost her.

Helen does not see Becky now, but she's been told Becky is not expected to live until morning. So Curtis and I are next. "Mommy!" Curtis cries out, "Grandma and Jimmy can fly just like birds! Can Grandpa and Grandma come live with us, Mommy? Because they don't even have a house, everything is gone!"

"Yeah, we'll figure out something." Helen does figure out a lot of things in the next weeks and months. She becomes our strength to go on. (I cannot even begin to imagine the pain Helen was feeling as she walked through the hospital learning the fate of her children, and the rest of her family.)

"And then they left me, Mommy. I hollered and hollered to Grandpa but they just drove away." (My little nephew, Curtis, how he must have felt right then, with Grandpa, and all of us, just leaving him, just breaks my heart.)

Helen consoles her little boy as best she can. "Curtis, your little sister Celi is in heaven, and God might want to take Becky too."

Curtis thought for a second, "I hope He doesn't, Mommy, but if He does, we'll just have to try to understand and be brave."

****

God didn't take Becky then, but her head had been badly injured. She was rendered unconscious for seven weeks, to awaken helpless as a newborn and to never fully recover mentally. But thick brunette hair came to cover her scars, and with bright eyes, though one blind, a clean and clear complexion, pretty smile and jolly laugh, she became our beautiful little girl anyway. She loved crafts, the music of CHARLIE PRIDE, and baking chocolate chip cookies for all her favorite men (me included!). She sometimes frustrated our attempts to communicate, but she always gladdened our hearts with her presence, until she died in her sleep in 1983, at 31.

We did get a house to live in, provided by Edwin Overboe of Kindred, North Dakota. Helen lived with us, nursed us, and her working husband, Clayton, joined us every evening. The Red Cross, churches, organizations, hundreds of families and individuals aided us and other storm victims who lost everything, giving food, money, countless hours of labor.

What happened with everybody's future I will share near the end.

Returning to the tornado experience, my family and I remember that terror, The Storm, that period in our history where everything else happened either before The Storm, or after. But now we have a comparison point, something to weigh against every other bad thing that could ever happen again. The experience instilled in me that bad things can and do happen, that they can be that bad, so I try not to take good things for granted. For fifty-four years I have experienced only rare days without remembering.

****

Two weeks after The Storm, after my cuts and bruises were well on their way to healing (I was hurt the least, the worst being a sprained ankle) I would see what was left of the farm.

Nothing.

Rubble. Piles of splintered trees and boards. Unbelievably twisted machinery.

Helen and Clayton brought me. I sat between them in a 1950 Ford Coupe. Never could I have imagined the utter devastation. This place had been my playground, a storybook farm. I buried my face in Helen's side and cried. For months afterward many things would frighten me, even things unrelated to the weather. I guess I must have thought a tornado lurked around every corner. At the age of ten I *knew* my home was invulnerable to any threat. Now, fifty-four years later, I know that no home—in fact, *nothing*—is invulnerable.

Twice, about a mile distant and during stormy weather, I have seen what looked like huge whirlwinds (likely tornadoes that did not fully form) maybe two or three hundred feet high. Both times west of me, so, of course, had it been the real thing it would have came toward me, because vicious weather comes *from* the west, not the east. And both times they lasted just seconds. Twice more I have seen clouds directly overhead whirling and twirling, *boiling*, but no tail came down. Twice more I have seen tails hanging in the sky, far, far, up and away (A thousand feet high? Two thousand? More?) and not moving, just hanging there doing nothing, basically, and finally disappearing. Later I learn that they are what are known as cold weather funnels, that can, *possibly*, grow and become violent. Many more times I have seen clouds rolling and tumbling over and over each other, always from the northwest to the southeast. But never have I seen a live tornado, except on television. I guess I should count myself lucky. But still, whenever storm clouds darken the sky

I go outside and watch them, until rain or straight wind forces me inside. (I used to think that rain would mean the violence was over, but I guess that's not exactly true.)

And when the weather comes at night, if there's any sign of red or purple on the TV radar, and close to me, I cannot sleep. I keep watching through the window until the thunder and lightening is just distant noise. A few years ago National Geographic had an article about tornadoes (April 2004). On pages 18-19 there is a map of the US of variously-colored lines showing all known trails of tornadoes since 1950. If you look at North Dakota, notice in the southeastern corner the two straight yellow lines. Yellow means F4 and F5, the biggest and meanest. One I'm sure represents the Fargo tornado in 1957. (One of the most heart-breaking photographs I've ever seen appears later in The Forum newspaper: A rescue worker holding the body of a small child, one of six children killed and all in the same family.)

The other yellow line I'm pretty sure represents *my* tornado: the 1955 Walcott tornado. What I'm trying to get to here is that I've watched the formation and dissolution of dozens, maybe hundreds of storms in these years since 1955. And many times I have been frightened—yes, frightened, maybe not terrified but *frightened*—watching, these, freaks, of nature. So why do I do it? Why don't I just take shelter and wait it out? I'll tell you why. Because if one of these freaks of nature is trying to kill me again I want to see the mutherfucker coming!

Sorry to stray so far from my story, but when stuff comes out it comes out.

Neighbors and friends and other volunteers had found and buried the dead livestock, mostly little pigs, some found hanging in trees. No kitties survived. And the cows and horses survived simply because they had been far to the north in the pasture. A friend, Volney Stevens, I heard, found and buried Pal, and marked her grave with the leg from a blue wooden chair. I looked but I never found her grave.

We—Dad, Mother, Gerry, and I—would return in October. We would rebuild in the same spot, with all the buildings just where they had been. Actually the only new building would be the barn. The hog house and granary (looking very much like the ones destroyed) would be found on other farms and moved in. Our house would come from a kind man from Sheldon, North Dakota. (I'm sorry, sir, but I don't know your name.) Cleanup would go on for years, but we did recreate a storybook farm. I say "storybook" because that farm had everything.

The approximately 10-acre farmstead was located directly on the boundary of east and west. East of the house was the new calf pasture, about three acres of green grass and boxelder trees growing from the roots still left in the ground from the mature grove that had been there. East beyond the calf pasture was flat agricultural field land.

Approximately 100 feet west of the house began the pastures and hay meadows. Native grass, wildflowers, wild animals, and hills.

****

The new barn became a magic place for me. A bull pen was located in the northwest corner, with a new bull every year. We always had three purebred Holstein bulls, a days-old calf, a yearling, and a two-year-old taking care of the cows. We were slowly developing a purebred dairy herd. The bulls were named after the farmer where we got them. Several were named Frank, one Dell, and one Terry. Dairy breed bulls are known for being mean, but they all respected the whip. They didn't seem to understand that the little whip we carried would mean nothing if they were to charge. Three calf pens held calves of different ages. An enclosed room held ground oats and corn for feed. Another room held a small machine that separated raw milk into skim milk—which we fed to the young calves, cats and dogs, and piglets—and cream, which we sold.

The south side of the barn held about a dozen stalls, one for each of the milk cows: Red, Knothead, Domino, Snowflake, Cutie-face, Keyhole, Brutus, Sparkle, Mabel, Chief Kickapoo, and Tiny, a dear little Guernsey with horns. Nearly every animal had a name. The cats were Major (a bobcat/domestic cross), Currents, Halloween, Patches, Puff, Frisky, Tommy, and Sylvester. Even some of the pigs had names (but naming forty piglets became a chore).

I had four bottle lambs one year. They were provided by Alder Helling, a dear neighbor. They became bottle lambs either because they were too weak to nurse properly or their mother would reject them. I gave them Indian names from THE SONG OF HIAWATHA by HENRY WADSWORTH LONGFELLOW.

No creatures on earth ever gave me so much trouble. Imagine having just two hands but four lambs all wanting to get fed at the same time. Normally I didn't have help. I don't remember how I handled it. Because, basically, only one could get fed at one time, because the nipple would not stay on the bottle unless you held it on, and of course the lamb is bunting the bottle (and me), because instinct is telling him/her that bunting will increase the milk flow. And had I and the bottle been its natural mother with an udder then his/her instinct would have been correct. There were several cuss words and much spilled milk. But I loved them.

And they wouldn't stay in their pen (which was built for the much bigger calves). The instigator was always the black-faced one I called Nokomis. Nokomis was the leader of the lambs and also a leader in the poem of HIAWATHA. But I strongly believe that if Nokomis hadn't been there one of the others would have led.

And of course there were more dogs: Sport, Tornado, Queenie, King, but no dog to this day has ever taken the place of Pal.

And I kept wild creatures: a horned lark, a great horned owl, a raccoon, a cottontail, white-footed mice, galvanized tubs for aquariums and terrariums. And nature visited our farm: crows, magpies, ducks and geese, great blue herons, minks and weasels, deer, fox, rabbits and squirrels. And right there on the farm I had 160 acres of trees, pastures, shelterbelts, wetlands, to explore. If I wanted to walk west I could go for miles and miles and never see another human being or habitation.

I was happy. I was satisfied. I loved my life. But I guess I wasn't really learning much *about* life. Because then teenage confusion set in.

****

I spent my first eight school years in a one-room country schoolhouse just a half mile from home. (Only twelve kids in all eight grades.) (The schoolhouse blew away too. A witness said it was way up in the sky and then just exploded. That fall another one-room schoolhouse was moved in.) I walked every day. I explored the ditches on both sides of the road. I found shiny pebbles and collected them. I found caterpillars of all colors and collected them, and put them in bottles with weeds, and watched them continue eating, then spin a cocoon, and in the spring come out as a butterfly or moth.

Then I graduated from eighth grade. The next year meant the town school. It meant riding a bus to school instead of walking. And meeting new kids. I don't really know what happened. I went from twelve kids in eight grades to 100 kids in twelve grades. It was different. It was a social shock. I didn't adjust.

I did fairly well my freshman year. I loved school and learning, especially my biology class, and Mr. Lensingrave who took us on a field trip, only about one or two blocks down the gravel road and ditch, but Mr. Lensingrave knew the names of plants and other stuff! And Mrs. Lahren's English class. I already loved to read, but she introduced me to the wonders of reading fiction. My favorite novel became SWIFTWATER, by PAUL ANNIXTER. For many years I would read that novel again and again. Thank you, Mrs. Lahren.

Then came the sophomore year. I started learning that some students didn't share my appreciation of school and learning. Some disrupted class, and gave the teacher a bad time, and did mean things to other kids. Once at physical-ed one of my best friends got his clothes torn off, right in front of everybody, boys and girls both. I was abhorred, and shocked, and can still see him walking naked. Another time a girl (not at school) got her clothes torn not off, just lifted so everybody cold see under her dress. She fought but had no chance. I was there but I couldn't (at least "didn't") protect her. I couldn't/didn't help or protect either. I still feel guilty about that. Some of you reading this might wonder, was that why I quit school, because I was afraid bad things would happen to me? I don't know but I don't think so. I don't remember ever being afraid, exactly, and also no bad things ever did happen to me.

Then I asked a girl to a rare school dance. She said "No," that her dad wouldn't let her go. That's what she said, but what I guess I must have heard, "No, I just don't want to go with you." I'm not saying that straw broke the camel's back either, but at the end of the sophomore year I announced I was quitting school. Others said they would too. But I was the only one who did. One of those who didn't quit that year quit the next, after his junior year.

Mr. Deinhart, my history teacher (who just had to announce it to the whole class one day when I got a hundred percent on a test) came out to the farm to see me, and tried to convince me not to quit. Thanks for that, Mr. Deinhart. I won't forget you.

After quitting school I took my very first job. Picking and grading potatoes for $1.00/hour. Wow, my first money. I soon bought a 1948 Chevy for $75.00. (And no, I don't still have it.) I was only fifteen and I was the only boy in my ex-class to have a car. Big deal. (A 1954 Ford would soon follow, and, no, I don't still have that either, and that was one cherry car!)

My next job was doing chores for our nearest neighbor while he received surgery for a hernia. For $25.00/week I worked from seven in the morning to about six at night, with a few hours off during mid-day. I read two nature books by Justice WILLIAM O. DOUGLAS that winter. MY WILDERNESS & MY WILDERNESS, EAST TO KATADIN. The neighbor's name was Randolph and his wife Rachel. They were one of the three neighbor families who I considered extra parents. Roger and Harlan were their sons. We grew up together and played lots of cowboy and Indian. Maxine was their sister. Occasionally, while doing chores for her dad, I got to see Maxine in the distance. But we didn't do anymore kissing.

I had several more jobs, all for neighbors and local farmers. Then I turned seventeen and that teenage confusion did not let up. In May of 1962 I gave up that heaven-on-earth storybook farm and went to see the local recruiter in Wahpeton, North Dakota. Soon I would be earning $85.00/month. Wow. But if I thought going to the "town" school was a social shock, I was in for a much ruder awakening.

7

CLASS A SCHOOL

But that rude awakening is now past. I have matured, somewhat.

From boot camp it's home for a two-week leave. What I remember from that leave was disappointing my mother that I was smoking. The other thing I remember was that I couldn't stay. I had to go back to the Navy.

I'm in the Navy now.

I remember not one other thing that happened during those two weeks, just that I wore my uniform a lot and thought I was pretty cool.

Next came Class A School. We were given three choices in boot camp as to what we wanted our naval career to be all about. I chose photography, meteorology, and ordnance. And in that order. (I got introduced to meteorology by the late DEWEY BERGQUIST, WDAY, FARGO, and his radio show DEWEY'S FOLLIES, in the early fifties, before The Storm, so I was younger than ten [see how a young child can be influenced?] After The Storm we finally got a TV so I got to see Dewey do the weather show. I rarely missed watching him.) Sorry. I really got side-lined there. Anyway, I got ordnance.

If I had put ordnance first I have to wonder if I would have gotten one of my other choices. Not likely. Ordnance meant returning to San Diego where I'd be right next door to the Naval Recruit Training Center. But I was no longer in boot camp. Now I had two stripes. I was a Seaman Apprentice! (E-2) An automatic advancement just for graduating boot camp. It was the last automatic anything.

Here they had two Class A schools. Sonar Technology (the sonar girls). And Torpedo Technology (tubesuckers). I was going to be a Torpedoman's Mate! I finally got my macho wish. But I had no idea where I was going.

The rumor was going around that they needed volunteers for submarine duty. Well, they got $55.00/month extra for hazardous duty pay. That was something. So I volunteered. What that mainly got me was a whole lot of visits to the dentist. I think they drilled and filled every tooth in my head. They also gave me advice on brushing my teeth. I had to buy six toothbrushes so that each one would dry out completely before I used it again. That didn't make any sense to me at all. But the day of my next visit I did buy six toothbrushes and got them all wet. Unfortunately, they were still wet when the dentist inspected them. Did I really think he wouldn't notice?

I didn't get punished for that though. We no longer got instant adolescent physical punishment. Our punishment now was mess duty or clean up. I did get extra mess duty once but I don't recall what for.

Here I got introduced to gamboling. Game of choice: Casino. I played for awhile. Lost lots of money. In fact when I left that base I still owed both Wyngrin and Petacki. I had to borrow the money from my dad on my next leave and mail it to them. Fuckers.

Took plenty of liberty. Went to lots of movies with Burris and Burrus and Larry E. Lagle, from Indiana, my best friend at Torpedoman School. I would run into him again on the USS Carbonero. The two of us were relaxing back on the Carbonero's fantail listening to the radio the day President Kennedy was shot. I Spent a lot of time at San Diego's YMCA, did a little dancing there. But there were always ten guys for every one gal. In the distance I heard about some guys taking drugs. I had no idea what kind of drugs they were taking, and why, if they weren't even sick, but it didn't really sound like the thing to do. So I didn't. And I hadn't even heard of marijuana yet—I hadn't even had my first beer yet. Hell, I was still only seventeen.

I was young. I was naive. I still am.

But I was macho. I was going to be a torpedoman!

I remember names and faces of three of my instructors. Chief Bell, Chief Draper, First Class Petty Officer Raspberry (E-6): "Boys, we're going to teach you how to kill." (Raspberry is also the one who mentioned "Choker" Thomas.)

But that 'killing' statement was pretty broad. Yes, the explosion from a torpedo would kill, but it would not quite be the same as the bullet from a gun or the point from a bayonet. Navy killing was different, but still killing.

We got four weeks of basic electricity, four weeks of basic electronics, four weeks of weapons. Yup, you guessed it. Somewhere in basic electronics I failed a major test and got set back again. Only this time there was no Hell's Island Bridge to cross. Just a simple setback to another class. For a time I wasn't certain whether they'd simply set me back or if I'd get kicked straight out to the surface fleet. I didn't want the surface Navy, I wanted the submarine Navy. I wanted that extra pay. It must have been scare-tactics. For they set me back to another beginning class to start all over again.

Again.

It was here (weapons class) that I failed my third personnel inspection. My first inspection in full dress blues, conducted by the chief weapons instructor. I remember his face (another rugged KIRK DOUGLAS type). But not his name. He looked me over. Then he looked at my shoes. He didn't smile. No inspecting officer ever smiled. Well, my shoes were spit-shined to the tone of black diamonds, but there was something else wrong. They were cracked. Not *cracked* cracked, like worn out. No. But you could see the creases. You know, where the shoe has to bend when you walk. I got extra duty for that, don't remember what. Nothing too serious. But after that I bought a new pair of shoes and kept them shined and stored just for inspections.

I celebrated my eighteenth birthday there and my first Christmas away from home. It was one of those humid, misty, rainy, chilly, San Diego nights. I had outside barracks watch. I carried an M-1 with live ammunition (not loaded, of course) and walked my beat in the loneliest place I had ever been in the world. In the darkness I could see huge ships—with their red and green side-lights—moving next door on San Diego bay. I mean the oceanfront was right there. I heard their mournful foghorns, and every one made the homesick bell toll. After about two hours had passed (the watches were four hours) the roving patrol came around. A Third Class Petty Officer (E-4). Whether he was a fellow torpedoman or a sonar girl I don't remember. What I remember is that he took my rifle and told me to go inside and warm up for a few minutes and have a smoke. I did. I went inside and sucked that cigarette for all it was worth, so hard and fast it made me dizzy.

The test for seaman (E-3) happened there. I had to pass a written test and do a few practical factors: Knots were one. I learned the square knot, the round turn and two half hitches and the bowline, which gave me a little trouble. One of my classmates made it easy and I still use the technique today. First make a loop, lay the loose end over your thumb, and (and this is what makes it easy) the rabbit (the loose end) comes out of the hole, around the tree, and goes back in the hole again. And tighten. There, you have a loop and a knot that will never come untied.

One more interesting thing happened at Class A school. "Interesting" might be a poor word. "Rite of Passage" is probably better. You remember Clint, that he would take me to Tijuana, right? Well, he did more than take me there. He also took me to my first whorehouse. I don't know what he did while I was busy. He probably was busy too. She was pretty, I guess. The room was small and well lit. It had a table that reminded me of an examining table in a doctor's office. She had me scoot up on there, lay down, then she pulled my jeans down, not off, just down, then my skivvy shorts, then she wrapped a towel (no messes) around my already well-erected 'peter' as she called it, "Nice big peter to suck."

Then (with no foreplay at all!) she went right to work. I don't remember how long I lasted. Not long. I don't remember my first fellatio as being particularly enjoyable, just quickly over. I don't think she thought it would be over so quickly either, as she soon was choking and coughing, "You cum in my mouth!"

Well, it wasn't my fault. She's supposed to be the professional. Right? Didn't Clint tell her I was a virgin? Maybe not. He probably thought I wasn't. So ended my first sexual escapade. Not exactly disappointing...exactly. The next escapade wouldn't come for a full year. Not until Yokosuka, Japan.

After Class A school I get another two-week leave. I go home, back to the farm, but don't remember one thing about that second leave either, except that, again, I couldn't stay. I had to return to the Navy.

I'm in the Navy now.

On one (or both) of those first two leaves I do remember something. I got a hug from my dear little niece, Patti, who likely was about five or six then. And also from my nephew, Michael, also about five or six. At that time he still called me Uncle Dimmy. I'm sure I got hugs from other nieces and nephews, too, but those two I remember, maybe because they were at that special, special, age.

And something was not quite right with my new orders. Instead of going to Submarine School in Connecticut, I was to report to Guided Missile Unit #10 at Pearl Harbor, Hawaii. A let down but there was nothing I could do about it.

8

FIRST DUTY

GMU10 maintained the quickly outgoing Regulus Guided Missile. It was launched from submarines, but the sub had to surface in order to launch. Not like the new Polaris. I remember hating being stuck on dry shore duty, playing lots of pool, and one name and face: Plante. Nothing personal, Plante, but I sure hated it there.

On about the tenth day at my new duty station the Executive Officer called me to his quarters, opened my service jacket, pointed out my request for submarines and informed me there was a sub in port with a billet for a torpedoman, "Do you want it?"

"Yes, sir! Thank you, sir."

The very next day in dress whites with loaded sea bag, I stepped onto the gangplank, walked halfway down, smartly saluted the stern flag, then saluted the topside watch, and reported aboard the USS Carbonero SS337. At last. The beginning of my naval career.

9

SKYDIVE!

How about we jump from my naval career again so I can tell you about another one of the important events in my life, OK? OK.

Several years have passed, I don't remember what year, mid-nineties, maybe, but I was in my late forties, or, I might have been fifty. And at any time, even now, about fifteen years later, I can still feel that wind, I can still be up there, still coming down, still seeing my friends leave that plane, one at a time.

And these were good friends, probably the best crew I ever worked with. The company, in Wheaton, Minnesota, manufactured power strips. We had the night shift, 7 P.M. to 7 A.M., twelve hours of bonding. And bond we did and we listened to 70's Classic Rock on 107.9 THE FOX! From Bruce "I love rock and roll!" When my time came to leave the company these friends surprised me with a going away party, including a cake and card signed by everyone, and several gifts, including an antique book, a hand-painted antique fruit jar, and a six-pack of MILLER GENUINE DRAFT. Oh yeah, and nearly endless hugs from the girls, even a few guys.

On breaks we went outside to smoke and talk and huddle in the cold. At some point in that circle of friends the word 'skydive' came up. As time went on it came up again and again, until we were actually making plans. But first came a three-day canoe trip on the Crow Wing River near Sebeka, Minnesota. We rented three canoes. Bruce and Chris in one, Kevin and Kraig in another, me in the third. I wanted to re-experience an earlier trip on the same river alone. I'll expand on that later if it fits in somewhere.

The thing about the canoe trip, we knew we had to do the *easy* thing first. If we had done the skydive first I fear it would have been difficult for our adrenalin counts to come back down for a canoe trip.

Brad leaves the plane first, but he's so dang big. Not much room under that wing. Be careful, Brad. See you on the ground, Brad. He's gone. The departure of his weight causes the small plane to heave upward. I don't see his fall. I can't see really well out the windows, and right now I'm too scared to want to.

Pat next. A calm expression. What's the matter with him? Why doesn't he look how I feel? His first time even in a plane. He tells me later he yoga-breathed from the time he entered the plane until he stepped out the door.

Now Chris. I pat the front of his right shoulder. He pats my hand. It could be the last time we see each other. He knows it too, and he's scared too (he says later: "When I was out on that wing, I didn't even know my own name!") but there's a grin a mile wide on his face.

Some still-functioning part of my brain is recording these dreamlike events, but I wonder what my face looks like.

Chris is away.

I'm alone, except for Pilot Ardell, and Jumpmaster Brian.

The plane begins another turn.

Jumpmaster Brian turns my way.

I'm next.

This skydiving sport can be dangerous. Even deadly. (Since my experience I have read several times of skydivers getting killed, when, *for some reason,* their parachute did not open, or maybe just opened badly.) For six weeks the six of us have talked. Brad says,

"There is an element of danger here." Has to be right the first time. At least close. Of course there's the emergency reserve chute, and the automatic-opening-device, which pops the reserve chute at 1200 feet, if you're dropping at least at 80 mph, and...you know, not cognizant.

Just in case....

At 3000 feet, where all first-timers begin, if nothing goes right, you reach the ground in thirty seconds.

But you don't think about whether your equipment will work. You assume it will. You put faith in it. You believe everything will go right, and you believe in your instructor, Don, who we've just spent the last eight hours with, learning and drilling.

And you believe in yourself. First you should believe you *want* to do this. Then you *must* believe you *can* do it. Don had us sign a paper too, saying we would hold no one else responsible if things didn't…you know, go right. That part was kind of upsetting to the old stomach, but we all signed.

"Move forward." The order comes from Jumpmaster Brian, with over 300 jumps. He has confidence in what he's doing, and in himself. He knows this sport is safe, and his confidence brims over to me.

I slide forward toward the open door.

I'm so scared. I'M SO, *FREAKING*, ***SCARED***!

Yet the fear, the real fear, is somehow somewhere else, on a back burner, far back in my psyche, because I am able to move forward.

Brian halts me partway and attaches my static line to an eyelet that is part of the plane. My ripcord will be pulled no matter what. What we did was not a true skydive but a static line parachute jump. Brian has me check the link too. Now all I have to do is get out of the plane. Even the pilot checks the link. It is secure. The pilot. I don't know him at all, have not even seen his face, but he is moving levers, pushing buttons, doing his job, flying the plane.

Now time to do my job.

“Get your feet out and stop.” Brian’s first major order, one of three. I barely remember hearing.

Training is thorough. Three to four hours of classroom, two to four in equipment usage. Don, one of the founders of VALLEY SKYDIVERS INC, West Fargo, North Dakota, put us through what sometimes seemed like unending drills: how to recognize failure in the main chute and what to do: The biggie. Also how to pull the reserve chute ripcord—if necessary—how to steer the canopy, how to land, and on and on.

I move further into the plane’s door, grasp the door casing and the floor casing, and ease my feet out—I’m petrified, yet doing what I’m supposed to—gradually finding a toehold on the tiny platform where I soon will be grasping for my life.

“Move all the way out.” Brian’s second command is what I’ve feared the most. But I can’t stop now. I won’t stop now.

I reach for the strut (the 45 degree support for the plane’s wing). Right hand secure. I thrust my body up, securing my feet on the platform, left hand also on the strut, then, hand by hand, leaning, I move outward, into 90-knot wind.

Fear does not exist right now. Nothing does. My mind is in total wooden shock.

I step into air to hang by my hands. No turning back now.

My next move would have been to look into my Jumpmaster’s eyes, to receive his last order: “Look up.” Looking up would have meant fixing on a red spot on the underside of the wing, for maybe a second, the purpose being to get into good body form: an arch, arms and legs spread-eagled, head back. Head back or you’ll go into a

dangerous somersault...

But something is wrong.

Things happened so fast that I can’t recall, exactly. (You have probably experienced that slow-motion sensation during an emergency.) But I think: The instant my weight (only about 115 pounds) went onto my shoulders I felt pain in the left one so sharp that it cut through everything and left me hanging by one arm.

So I let go. I remember a fading glimpse of the plane and Brian's face as I fall away. I don't feel the jerk from the ripcord. I have no comprehension at all of what's happening.

But I know I got my head back because the next thing I remember is seeing that glorious orange-and white chute above me. OPEN! Catching air, slowing my descent. The training and drilling worked!

But all is still not well.

The cascade lines have several twists, probably the easiest situation to correct. But my left arm hangs limply, hurting. But the twists must come out, and the slide (a nylon rectangle separating you and the parachute's risers from the cascade lines) must come down, so the chute will stabilize and open fully.

But there's time.

But not forever. First, untwist the lines.

Somehow my left shoulder works and I grasp the rear risers, and kick out in the opposite direction of the twists.

And, just as Don said, the twists come out and the cascade lines jerk free. Thank you, God. Although I don't remember thanking God.

Still the riser. Is it down? I don't really remember knowing. But the steering toggles have to come down. Somehow my left shoulder works again. I'm able to pull both toggles off the Velcro, and for now just hang on.

And enjoy the view. And, God, oh, God, it is beautiful, it is so beautiful. Checkerboard fields, the winding Sheyenne River, the cities of Fargo and West Fargo.

"Number four, hold your position." Or something like that. It's Don on the ground, speaking to me on a one-way radio hanging from my neck. We went in by numbers, not names. First in, last out. I'm Number Four. So I hold position, at half-brake, drifting south with no cares.

Time passes. I don't remember thinking, just seeing the beauty. Even the pain seems far away. The jumpsuit fits well; a glance reveals an abundant cavity under my left shoulder blade, kind of a gruesome sight, but no worrying about it now.

Just enjoy the ride down. The West Fargo airport is below. Hangers left, runway straight down, to the right sewage lagoons...don't want to land there though.

"Hard left, Number Four."

A 180 degree turn, to face into the wind and slow the 20 mph forward chute speed. My left hand has been grasping the steering toggle a little above my head, which evidently has created a makeshift sling, because the pain has been forgotten, but now I must pull the left toggle clear down to my groin.

I don't know how my shoulder works but I make the turn.

"Hard left, Number Four."

Please, let me turn right. But, of course, Don doesn't know my left shoulder is dislocated, so, again, but with pain I'll never forget, I turn south, again. Still directly over the airport.

"Hard left, Number Four."

Once more, but I'm close now. I see Chris below, gathering his chute. I'll land a little north of him. Not the feather-landing on my feet I had planned—in fact I have no legs, I'm exhausted, and get a graceless slide on my butt onto wet grass, and all I want is attention for my shoulder.

My arm is almost useless now but still I gather the chute and start in. Jumpmaster Brian, already landed, meets me halfway. He has noticed I'm not exactly swaggering. Pat comes out too. Both will accompany me as Brad hauls me to MERITCARE Emergency Room, all three becoming something of heroes to me.

There are two divers in our group left to go up, Kraig and Sondra, and I hope my pained appearance does not stop them. It doesn't. I don't get to see their ride but a call from the emergency room confirms they are both safe back on the ground.

At the emergency room endless questions and waiting, then Dr. Keske arrives and shows me the x-ray. No part of my upper arm ball rests in the socket. I expect worse pain...but, almost none. With my arm raised above my head Dr. Keske puts one finger in my armpit and nudges.

A soft klunk and instant relief. Another hero.

Later I sit alone. I feel like crying. Tears do get close. Why? I'm not sure. No more fear or pain. That's all past. I think the tears are of great relief, and lofty feelings of triumph. I didn't completely win but I didn't get beat either. And many people have helped me, and friends are near.

Three flash memories have stayed strong: The last glimpse of the plane and Jumpmaster Brian, a whoosh as if going under water, and then an eruption and realization of the chute open. But no memory of the two to four seconds between. I've wondered if blackout occurred, and what the others remembered. Chris: "Freefall" even "Tumbling." Brad and Pat: "Nothing." Sondra, our gutsy little blonde, with horsewoman femininity rounding out our circle of human bonding: "Blanked out." Kraig perhaps said it best: "Your mind just couldn't accept what was happening."

Would I do it again? I don't know. The shoulder took time to heal. If I did it again it would be what they call a tandem jump, where I would be attached to the front of an experienced diver. (You know, the kind President H.W. Bush has done at least twice, maybe three times, in his eighties no less.) I know the fear would return, but so would that indescribably awesome rush of adrenaline, and, eventually, if confidence and skill is attained, that climb to 10,000 feet and the two-minute freefall ride at 120 mph, seeing the world as it can be seen no other way.

****

I did go back about a year later, with a camera. I wanted some photographs to illustrate the article that was to appear in THE FORUM, Fargo, North Dakota. I got my wish but I couldn't just ride in the plane. I had to also wear a parachute and get buckled into the door, in fact a part of my body would actually hang out of the plane, and we were going to 10,000 feet, where the professional skydivers would jump from. I was a bit nervous getting buckled in, "You won't fall out," Ardell said, "Trust me."

Right. I trust you.

And I did get some good action photographs, but when my photos came back I discovered that my dependable Fujica had chosen that day to stop advancing the film. Every photo had about three exposures—ARRRRRRRGH!

At this time I would like to thank the late editor, JOE DILL, of THE FORUM, Fargo, ND. He not only approved the publishing of both my tornado story and the skydive story, but also gave me encouragement to keep writing. Thanks, Mr. Dill.

10

USS CARBONERO

Back to the Navy.

Several months after arriving I am still stuck on board with no liberty. I am what is referred to as a nonqualified puke and not just that but a *delinquent* nonqualified puke, and lower than whale shit. I should try to explain how low whale shit is: From one old salt: "It's the only thing big enough and heavy enough to sink to the bottom of the ocean!" Of course that's not exactly a scientific viewpoint, but it satisfied me.

By nonqualified I mean I wasn't yet "qualified". By delinquent I mean I was behind in my studies. Hey, after all I didn't get submarine school, so I was behind when I started. And all that means I didn't yet know how to operate every valve, didn't know what every switch was for, I hadn't crawled every square inch of those oily bilges checking out where every pipe and wire went to and what they did. I hadn't yet slammed open the valve that blew Bow Buoyancy so we could surface. I hadn't yet transferred water from one tank to another so we kept our trim. It meant that I was a nonqualified PUKE. I hadn't yet earned my dolphins. And until I did—until I could perform every job of every other man in that boat, so that I could do it if I was alone in an isolated compartment and we were flooded, burning, sinking, and the lives of every other man aboard depended on me—I would remain a nonqualified PUKE.

Emphasize the word "PUKE."

This was important.

Being qualified is necessary.

To wear those dolphins will be godlike.

But we are going to be visiting Bora Bora.

Bora Bora is one of the Society Islands including Tahiti.

And we will be far from any official Navy.

So the rules are waived.

I am allowed to go ashore, but under escort. "Escort" sounds pretty military. There is no official escort. But I have to wear regular dungarees whereas everybody else could wear civilian clothes. And I do go with two or three other guys who I'm pretty sure are under unofficial orders to keep me out of trouble.

The beer in Bora Bora, at least then, was dark, thick as a milk shake, and came in I swear two-quart bottles. I "might" have started my third one before it was all over. But, hey, guys, this is only the second time I've tasted beer (or alcohol of any kind) in my life. The first time is a story I'll get to.

I remember a couple of things from Bora Bora. While I was on this unofficial liberty, drinking beer in this bamboo/straw hut on this fabulously green and tropical faraway island in the South Pacific, there appeared this very, very, beautiful young girl, the dream of every sailor. She was Polynesian, had hair the color of black oil, bronze skin and filled to the brim with body. And all of fifteen or sixteen. If that. A child. At least how I've been brought up to think of as a child. I think she spoke to me, but I was well on my way to oblivion. All I remember for sure is that she was beautiful and she was there.

The other thing I remember is when we were leaving Bora Bora. There is this rule that, when leaving port, the sanitary tanks are blown (emptied). I think everybody can guess what "sanitary" means so I won't elaborate. The thing is it's done before we get underway, that is, right beside the pier. I remember that clear water. We could see the bottom, at least twenty or thirty feet down. Suddenly here comes that cloud of, well, yeah, shitty water, from the bottom of the boat.

But I got ahead of myself. Many adventures and frustrations come on the Carbonero before Bora Bora.

****

Immediately my nickname is "Nelly." It has been from day one in the Navy. Different people, same nickname. But here on the Carbonero I earn some new ones. Already on my first trip home I notice I'm getting a high forehead. I'm only seventeen, damn it! But baldness has started. Yes, it's probably only normal male pattern baldness but I choose to believe it was caused by that mutherfuckin' white hat. Before the Navy I never wore anything on my head except when working on the farm. In boot camp it had to be screwed down tight, always, everywhere except inside a building. So, my new nicknames become Baldy, Chrome Dome, others I can't think of but all referring to my receding hairline.

Later I earn other nicknames that have to do with a different part of the body. I'll touch on that later.

Even though my first priority is getting qualified I also must perform regular military duties. Watches: Topside with a holstered . 45 caliber semi-automatic pistol while in port, Lookout while on the surface at sea and Bow and Stern Planesman while dived below. And Helmsman on both the surface and dived.

The first thing I do at sea is get seasick, from which I never fully recover. From the moment that last hatch closes, and the boat starts to sway and lean, and the smell of diesel fumes hits me, I'm seasick. It'll last from days to weeks every mutherfuckin' last time.

When I think of it right now it occurs to me that the diving alarm sounds a lot like somebody puking. But diving made me recover from seasickness, only to get sick again when we surfaced.

Marshall is my instructor for helmsman, lookout and planesman. He is a poster sailor if I ever saw one. Tall and slim. Blonde crewcut. Clean-shaven, always, even if we had been at sea for three weeks. He looked sharp no matter what uniform he wore. Dress whites, dress blues, dungarees. He probably went on to become a Navy recruiter.

The officer of the deck (OOD) for my first dive is Mr. Anderson, Lieutenant JG (Junior Grade), O-2, the second rank for officers in the Navy. He has silver dolphins because at some point in his career he had qualified as an enlisted man, but then had risen to the officer ranks. But he didn't yet have his gold dolphins, so, in a way (a very vague way) he is like me.

Nonqualified.

We are on the bridge somewhere at sea near Hawaii. The bridge on a World War II diesel submarine is not a very big place. Room for about six people if they don't mind being crowded. Plus two pukas (openings in the superstructure that allows the lookout to poke his head up.) We are out for about two weeks for normal operations. Training, war games, you know. I have the starboard lookout. It's night. Marshall has already told me everything I need to know to be a lookout: "Surface contact ten degrees off the starboard bow, amidships-right, starboard side (ninety degrees), dead ahead (zero degrees), dead astern (180 degrees), amidships left, port side (270 degrees); and he told me how to report aircraft, whales, Japanese fishing balls, sea bats...and if I couldn't clearly see an object at night, I should look a little above and to the right (or was it left?). Anyway that worked, and I've used that technique of sighting distant objects at night ever since.

Soon the OOD will say "Clear the bridge." And we will be diving. I am nervous about that. Not about actually going beneath the surface of the Pacific Ocean with likely a couple of miles of water still beneath us (I never worried about going down and not coming up; that was something one shouldn't think about if one wanted to be a submariner). No, what worries me are those two ladders I have to get down, first to the Conning Tower (where the periscope is), then on down to the Control room...with two other guys coming down *right* behind me.

The starboard lookout goes first, then the port lookout, then the OOD. Upon arrival in Control, the starboard lookout pushes the start switch for the bow planes, then jumps left and pushes the start button for the stern planes and becomes the stern planesman. And the port lookout becomes the bow planesman. And the OOD stands right between us telling us what depth he wants from the bow planesman and what degree bubble he wants from the stern planesman.

"No problem," Marshall assures me, and goes on to demonstrate. I watch as he grips the handrail of that ladder, jumps, grips the same handrail with his feet, and drops smoothly to the Conning Tower deck beside the helmsman, makes an about-face, then pulls off the same feat with the longer Control Room ladder. A pro. He should have been a stuntman in the movies.

He comes back up. "Now you do it, Nelly." Right.

Adrenalin already was getting its grip on me. Funny thing about adrenalin. Suddenly you can do something you thought you couldn't. And if you do it wrong you don't notice, and if you get hurt, well, you feel it but it doesn't really register as pain until later. And the really funny thing about adrenalin is—at least in my viewpoint—you go into slow-motion.

The slow-motion part doesn't happen on my trial clearing of the bridge. I don't even remember the trial part. I just do it, then climb back up to the bridge to await the real thing. Which isn't long in coming.

"Clear the bridge!"

RrrUuuuugha! RrrUuuuugha! (See? I told you it sounded like somebody puking.)

I tuck my binoculars under my arm, grab the ladder, jump and feel my feet grab the ladder, and hit the deck of the Conning Tower. Then an about-face and grab the other ladder..."Dive! Dive!" comes a voice on the intercom.

That trip down from the bridge takes no more than a few seconds but becomes a flashpoint in my mind. I hit the Control Room deck, turn, punch the bow plane motor switch, hear the port lookout hit the deck no longer than one second after I had just been there, then I hit the start button for the stern planes and grab the stern planes wheel. (Like the helm and the bow planes wheel, 3-4 feet in diameter.)

The OOD hits the Control Room deck, and now becomes the Diving Officer, "Two degrees down bubble! Make your depth eight-five feet!"

This is the real Navy. No more bullshit like in boot camp and Class A School. This is the real thing. I'm in the Navy now!

Marshall has already given me instructions on the bow and stern planes operation too. But adrenalin has taken over. I have just been given an order. I jerk that stern planes wheel left (or was it right?). That bubble takes off like a raped ape; it goes way beyond two degrees down.

That's when I get the index finger in the ribs. "Get that bubble back, Nelly, goddamn it!" (Yes, Mr. Anderson calls me Nelly, too. Most of the officers use nicknames liberally. We are all together on this tiny boat, and not a lot of room for strict military rules.)

Anyway I chase that bubble. I jerk the wheel back, watch that bubble end its flight down, stop, then come zooming back in the opposite direction, past amidships, past two degrees up, and on and on. The stern probably came right out of the water on that dive.

Meanwhile, Mr. Anderson is giving orders to other sailors, and hearing statements about the condition of the sub.

"Green board, sir!" (All the hatches are closed.)

"Very well! Pump 5000 pounds from negative to safety." (These are tanks that hold sea water to give us positive or negative buoyancy. In an emergency safety tank would be blown. I don't remember exact amounts or which tank got what from where, but you get the idea...right?)

We reach eight-five feet (periscope depth). Bow planes are to control the depth, stern planes the up-angle or down-angle. We're drifting up.

"Ten dive," says the bow planesman.

Now I must compensate by going to five rise. If we do this correctly the bow planesman will bring us back down to depth and I will keep the angle level.

From the captain in the Conning Tower, “Make your depth 300 feet!”

“Full dive on both planes!” orders Mr. Anderson, “Flood negative!”

We seem to go down like a rock but steady out at 300 feet.

Another order comes down from the Conn, “Rig ship for silent running.” That means no unnecessary talking, no radio, and every unnecessary pump or motor gets turned off. That means air conditioning, too. It won’t be long before the air begins to stifle. (Sometime in the future, the longest we will go down without even snorkeling will be 24 hours [it becomes difficult to even keep a cigarette going.])

Mr. Anderson passes the order on. No, it won’t go out over the noisy intercom but the sound-powered phones. In every compartment right now a man sits with a headset on, his only job being to hear and relay messages.

Then comes the sound of distant explosions, make-believe depth charges. But too far away. We win this one. Sometime in the future we will operate with the Japanese Navy. They will drop those grenade-sized(?) make-believe depth charges right on top of us. The closeness of the explosions—maybe even the shiver of the boat—will leave no doubt in anyone’s mind that this one we did not win. Luckily, the Japanese today are staunch allies.

But, today we win. The order soon comes down from the Conn, from the Captain, “Secure from silent running. Make your depth eight-five feet. Make all preparations to surface.”

We make preparations.

From the Conn: “Take us up!”

From the Diving Officer, “Full rise on both planes! Blow Bow Buoyancy!”

Built like a mountain, Reeves, on the air manifold, cracks the Bow Buoyancy valve. A high pressure blast follows.

Air replacing sea water in the bow buoyancy tank gives us a

distinct up-angle. We secure the planes and get ready to follow the OOD back up to the bridge.

"Blow Main Ballasts! Sound the surface alarm!"

RrrUuuuugha! RrrUuuuugha! RrrUuuuugha!

We climb the Control Room ladder.

"Surface! Surface! Surface!"

Staley the Quartermaster, hands on the Conning Tower hatch wheel is awaiting his order.

"Crack the hatch!"

"Aye, Aye, Sir!"

From the Chief of the Boat (COB) in the Control Room, "Red light on the Conning Tower hatch, Sir!"

"Very well! Open it!"

Staley opens it, then steps clear. The OOD whips to the bridge, followed by the Port Lookout, then the Starboard Lookout (me), finally Marshall. What I remember from all those surfacings is the smell, the taste, the very feel of the sea air. And the sound of the sea water crashing against us and running in rivulets off everything...as if we had just been immersed in it. And, this time, the very close presence of other Navy ships, and naval aircraft trailing sonar buoys, buzzing us, maybe a little pissed that we had outmaneuvered them. This time.

OOD calls down the to helmsman, "All ahead two-thirds!"

The helmsman answers, "All ahead two-thirds, aye, Sir!"

The helmsman controls what direction the boat goes by turning the helm wheel, left for left rudder which turns us left, amidships, right rudder, etc. The speed order he passes to the Maneuvering Room by way of bells and twin dials with pointers.

Even from the bridge we hear the bells answer.

"Answers all ahead two-thirds, Sir!"

"Very well! Right full rudder!"

"Right full rudder, Sir!" Moving the rudder (or planes) hydraulically, does not take long, "Rudder is right full, Sir!"

"Very well, come right to 180 degrees."

Due south. We're headed home. Just a few days this first trip out for me. I've been seasick the whole time except when dived. And even the first time topside was too much. (Yes, I puked over the side while on my first lookout.) But that was the only time ever while topside.

When we arrive back in port a strange thing happens. When my feet hit solid ground it's as if the whole world moves. My feet at first want to stay where they are, but then my trunk wants to compensate for the way the world is *seemingly* moving, and then my feet have to move in order for me not to fall down. This...dance, continues for several seconds while my physical body adjusts to the fact that the world is not really moving. My poster sailor Marshall is there. After I at last stand up straight again he chuckles, "You've got your sea legs, now, Nelly."

That's the only thing I remember about Marshall. He was there for me during my first days and training at sea, and then he was there for me for my first steps back on dry land, and then he's gone from memory. But not forgotten.

****

Back to submarine qualification. Approximately twenty percent of the eighty-man crew is nonqualified. Yes, Carbonero is definitely a training ship. As we learn the different ship systems (fuel, electrical, hydraulics, electronics, tanks, bilges, etc.), first a qualified enlisted man must test our knowledge with questions and a check of our hand-drawn blueprint, then sign his initials. Then an officer must check. At some point I have gotten behind. Right. First I got behind in boot camp. Then I got behind in Class A School. And now I'm behind in submarine qualification. I'm delinquent. I'm a delinquent nonqualified puke. But nobody is threatening to kick me out. Just keep bearing down I'm told. But, you are going to pay for being behind. No more liberty.

Fine.

We're at sea most of the time anyway. But there is that Bora Bora trip coming up.

But first....

Navy subs have competing softball teams just like civilian companies. I don't get to play ball either. But then I've never cared that much for sports anyway. Except for things like shooting pool and roller-skating (which I learned to enjoy about in the fifth grade thanks to the prodding of my dear sister Gerry.) Pool I learned somewhere else along the line; first from farm neighbors who had a pool table in their basement, and then from a shark (a stranger) who —upon my arrival back in San Diego from boot camp leave—first drew me in with a couple losses, then turned into a shark and took some of my scarce money. Boy, he saw me coming a mile away.

Anyway, I wouldn't have minded *watching* softball.

But....

Mr. Anderson has taken a liking to me. (I wonder where he is today? Probably a retired fleet admiral. He deserved whatever good things happened to him. Another one of my teachers who I'm thanking way, way, late.) Anyway, I've been aboard for about three months now, most of that time delinquent, and Mr. Anderson has arranged for me, a delinquent nonqualified puke, to help his wife deliver beer to a softball game. I guess he figures I need some R&R. He's correct.

I don't remember a thing about the game. But that afternoon I have my very first beer. And then my second. Then my third...I don't know how many more I drank, likely not many—if any—but I'm soon drunk and pukin'. And I'm not even seasick. Pukin' from seasickness at sea and drunkenness in port.

I'm in the Navy now.

Mrs. Anderson delivers me back to the boat too. I doubt I was much help to her with the beer. Though I'm sure she had plenty of help. Thanks, Mrs. Anderson. What I remember about you is that you were very pretty and a very nice lady. I hope I didn't hit on you, not that I would have had a clue how to hit properly on a lady. Still true today.

****

Back to Bora Bora. While on the way we must cross the equator. We pollywogs must become shellbacks. It's the ancient law of the deep.

From the Captain: "All stop."

We have reached the equator. For days we have talked about the upcoming celebration and initiation. Only about eight members of the crew are shellbacks. Certainly we pollywogs should be able to hold our own against so few.

But we will have no chance for a frontal assault.

We are herded to the Forward Torpedo Room. We are ordered to strip down to just skivvy shorts. They will take us topside, one at a time.

The first guy goes up. We, of course, cannot see what happens to him. We can't even hear anything.

It's becoming a little scary. (I'm not kidding. It *did* become a little scary.)

My time comes.

I climb the ladder. I see Radioman Chief Elias sitting in judgment. We're all guilty. He's dressed like a pirate and not smiling. It's sunny. The sky is nearly cloudless. The sea is so calm. The water on the equator, today, is like glass. We should be celebrating this moment...and I guess we are.

I scramble on deck. I don't remember what Chief Elias says. He maybe says nothing. Nothing that could warn those still below. He maybe just points. King Neptune and his Queen are waiting. I stand before them. I'm officially pronounced guilty of my pollywog crimes. I must fall to my knees and kiss the royal baby's belly which is smeared with grease. (Fred Lund is the royal baby. I didn't forget ya, bud!)

There are pirate guards holding lengths of fire hose. There are a growing number of brand new shellbacks. There will be no argument. No escape.

I fall to my knees.

I hesitate mouthing that grease.

Then comes the first Whack on my bottom. And another.

I kiss that royal belly.

Another Whack! "Do it better!"

I kiss like I mean it.

I pass, and am escorted to a twenty-foot enclosed canvas garbage chute, coated (on the inside of course) with more grease...and the foulest, vilest, most vulgar, most disgusting and nastiest garbage that ever left a table. They must have saved it and stored it for weeks!

I must crawl through this bowel-like tunnel, this intestine that really, really, needs a good, strong, enema first.

I stare at it.

Whack!

I drop to my knees.

Whack!

That hurts. Whack! No more screwing around. Whack! I lift the edge—Whack!—drop to my belly—Whack! Whack!—and begin crawling—Whack! Whack! Whack!—no stopping, can't see, can barely breathe—Whack! Whack! Whack! I reach the other end. My head pops back into the sunshine. The whacking stops. I'm now a shellback.

Becoming a shellback instantly qualifies me to take up my own length of fire hose. I do, but my heart is not in this. (What the hell am I doing in the military?) The guy following me crawls into the tunnel. I give him a few light-hearted whacks. I hope it didn't hurt too much. I've done my duty. I return my fire hose to be used by the next newly initiated shellback. Then I only witness the ancient rite continue.

At its conclusion there are congratulations and feasting and cleansing. Many of the guys jump into the ocean for their first bath. I don't. Yes, they taught me how to swim in boot camp. Sort of. But no way will I jump into that Pacific Ocean. There is likely two or three miles, or more, of water below us, and the farther down one would go the darker it would get. Sometimes that bothers me, a little, that I'm a sailor, at sea, and I can't, really, swim.

It is sometime now, in 1963, that the USS THRESHER SSN-593, goes down. I think about those guys sometimes. What their last moments were like. They were a nuclear submarine, much newer than Carbonero. Their hull was thicker. They could go deeper, and they would, likely, have been much deeper when the hull collapsed. Death would have been very, very, quick. Did they even know it was coming? Did the Captain even know? Did the Diving Officer even have time to warn him? On the older boats, like Carbonero, the Captain is usually present for all dives. Because we don't make that many dives. But when the nukes go to sea they dive and stay dived. That's the beauty of nuclear power.

So it's possible only the Diving Officer—and the few men on duty in the Control Room right then—knew THRESHER was in trouble. How fast did it happen? What happened? Did the Diving Officer announce it to the crew? That they were going down? Did he even have time to consider announcing it? Would the men have wanted to know? Would I have? I don't know. I like to think I would have wanted to know. But would I have used that time remaining of my life to beg forgiveness from my god for my many sins and trespasses? Or would I have just sat, in shock? Waiting. Would I even have thought of my loved ones? I don't know.

But a submariner cannot think, seriously, of these things.

He can't let it bother him.

One guy I remember it bothered.

He was fresh from the surface Navy, gung-ho, and wanted to become a submariner. Submarine duty is strictly voluntary. He came to us and went to sea with us. I suppose he likely made at least one dive. I don't know what happened. What I do know is that operations came to a halt. A helicopter came out to us at sea and that surface sailor was put in a bucket and removed from Carbonero. He must have decided he really, *really*, didn't want to do this. So he had to go. In his likely frame of mind he would have become a danger to us all. I don't remember this guy's name. I wouldn't say it even if I did remember. Because this had to be one of the lowest moments in his naval career, maybe even in his whole life.

So we couldn't think about going down. Or even drowning. And I didn't. And I didn't consider myself brave. I still don't. But I just couldn't see myself dying that way…or *any* way for a long, long, time. Therefore, I wouldn't. So, I didn't think about it.

There was one time, though, that I remember getting a bit nervous. First I need to explain a couple things. A submarine's hull is surrounded by tanks, with valves on the bottom to let water in, and vents on top to let air out. (In the great movie, CRIMSON TIDE, with DENZEL WASHINGTON [he's been one of my favorite actors all the way back to the television series, ST ELSEWHERE.]; anyway, there is a good exhibition of what happens when a submarine submerges: Water and air from the vents shoots high above the superstructure.) On the surface the main ballast tanks are filled with air, therefore positive buoyancy. And fuel ballast tanks (about the same thing) are filled with diesel fuel, which keeps four diesel engines running. As the fuel is used it's replaced with "heavier" sea water. When a sub dives it needs negative buoyancy. The valves and vents open and sea water replaces air. Negative buoyancy in a hurry. But that's all planned for. The sailors remain in control.

But this one time…and I don't know all the details but will describe as best I can.

During this dive something happened to a fuel ballast tank. A valve ruptured, or a vent opened unexpectedly…like I said I'm not sure what happened, but a whole lot of diesel fuel got replaced with a whole lot of the much heavier sea water, which very quickly gave us a whole lot of extra negative buoyancy, and a steep down angle.

I was on watch in the After Torpedo Room. I remember sort of holding my breath, and when I did breathe they were short breaths, something like how I was breathing waiting for my turn to leave that plane. I don't remember thinking anything. No, I wasn't thinking of my loved ones, I wasn't thinking about God and death and my many trespasses. I really don't think I was thinking at all, just waiting. They were taking care of this emergency in the Conning Tower, the

Control Room, and Maneuvering, so, there was nothing for me to do but wait it out. (And, remember what I said earlier: I wasn't going to die like this.) And, of course, we didn't sink, because I'm here today writing about it.

I don't remember ever going below three hundred feet, but the depth gauge read seven hundred. I also don't remember if the gauge showed deeper than that or if there was a red line or something at seven hundred feet, signifying that much deeper would mean…?

I don't know, but for a time after that, a short time, I did consider that, yes, I did have kind of a dangerous job, but still it didn't sway me. I just knew I was not going to die like that. I had too much yet to do in life. And something was beginning to set in upon me. An affliction. I liked this life. I liked the action. The adventure. It seemed to be almost nonstop. Sure, there were slow times. But they were few. And I was changing. I didn't know then that I would have a difficult time readjusting to civilian life, what I especially didn't know was that *that* was the reason, that there would be no more adventure, nothing in my civilian life to compare with riding a submarine, and being a part of the United States Navy.

It was an honor then; it's an honor now; it will always be an honor.

I could, right now, take this moment to blame the Navy for me being so fucked up when I got out. My mother blamed the Navy. She said I was never the same again. And I wasn't. I had grown up, a little. But I hadn't matured. Maybe if I had waited a couple more years before enlisting. Maybe then I wouldn't have even enlisted. Maybe this. Maybe that. If I hadn't enlisted it would have changed my whole life. There are a thousand things I would not have done, but a thousand other things I would have done. Better things? Worse? I will never know. I do know there are very, very, few things that I have done that I would have done differently.

****

I would ride the Carbonero for about eighteen months more. I would become submarine qualified. Six months to the day, taking three months longer than most others. But that day would come when I lined up in my dress blues with several others topside on the USS Carbonero SS337, and Captain Jack Jarvies would come down the line, stopping at each newly qualified submariner, pin his dolphins on, step back and salute him, then look him straight in the eye and shake his hand, "Congratulations, Nelson!"

That was one of my proudest moments in the Navy. I finally had earned my dolphins. And what did I get for it? A toss in the drink. They did let me change into dungarees, though. We were somewhere other than Pearl Harbor. One of those other Pacific Islands. We were anchored instead of moored. When it happened it came quickly and unplanned, but suddenly there were four guys there, one on each of my extremities. (They did allow me to empty my pockets.) Second Class Torpedoman Petty Officers (E-5s) Richard Lynchwick and John Abare were two of them (I still luv ya, guys!) I don't remember the other two. (One might have been Roberts.) The thing is, each was big enough he could have thrown me in by himself. But no. Each one grabs an extremity, heave-ho's two or three times, then lets me go. I fly about thirty feet out into the harbor.

Oh, yeah. That's right. I can't swim really good. But we *are* in port. Hopefully they'll hang around to see if I get out, and if I don't they'll at least be able to drag the harbor and probably find my body. So I don't tell'em I can't swim good. I don't want to spoil the moment. My back-stroke does bring me back to the boat, where they pull me out.

That was a proud moment too. Sort of. They thought enough of me to throw me in. *And* pull me out.

There was another proud moment, or maybe another rite of passage. Neither of those terms describe it appropriately. Anyway, I turned twenty in Hawaii, the legal drinking age there, and my good shipmates threw a birthday party for me at the local Submarine Bar, and I'm sorry but I can't recall the name of that bar. The responsible ones I'm pretty sure were Dennis Staley, Quartermaster, Torpedomen Richard Lynchwyck and John Abare. I don't remember all who came but I'm pretty sure Timan, Engineman and Reynolds, Radioman, showed up. Thanks, guys!

****

Besides Bora Bora and Oahu (where Pearl Harbor is) we visited the Big Island of Hawaii, the Garden Island of Kauai, Olongapo Bay in the Philippines, Hong Kong (went ashore with Daniel O'Dwyer, Second Class Electronics Technician [E-5]), the islands of Midway, Kwajaline, Guam, and Sasebo, Yokohama, and Tokyo, Japan, and Yokosuka, where I would do sex in the missionary position and at last lose my cherry in the proper way. (All this happened inside two years.)

But first I'm going to tell Julia's story. She and her three beautiful daughters deserve this recognition from me.

11
JULIA'S STORY

Dear Julia...,

Julia was with us just fifteen days short of forty-two years. A very short time but she did a lot. She bore three lovely daughters and loved them intensely. She loved nature, wanted to be a forester, and planned to have a log cabin in the woods by the time she turned fifty: ("The farther into the boonies the better.") She loved photography, and created many memories with her camera. From her balcony she shared time with six-year-old Laura, her cat, Kennedy, and me on the phone. She loved and described the stars, the moon, the night sky. And she opened me to love again and gave me the best months of my life. Oh, yes, and she was beautiful. She didn't know it. She had no clue that she was beautiful. And from Maggie, her best friend at work, she "…tried so hard not to be noticed."

But she was noticed, and she left a big gap in many lives.

It's midnight, Julia, three weeks since your passing, and it's still so very unreal to me. You opened your arms to me and never closed them, and, after years of solitude, loneliness, locked doors, you caused my arms to open to you. But our time was so short—what the hell happened?

Five o'clock, Sunday, July 13, 1997.

We close down our work place. We've had a perfect day at work together. We've hugged every half hour. We're happy. After our minor spat last night we're more in love than ever.

But there's that old fact of you being late. Always. I say, "Please don't make me wait till eleven o'clock tonight."

"I won't," Julia returns. She'll move Laura from one babysitter to the next and will get back, "About five-thirty," she says.

Well, even perfect me couldn't do it that quickly. So, I will rent the movie we've been planning to watch, FALLING DOWN with MICHAEL DOUGLAS, and then go to the parking lot where we usually meet, to wait for her. We'll eat together, then go home just as planned.

Six o'clock arrives. OK, Julia, you've had about enough time.

Six-fifteen. Where are you, Julia? Six-thirty. I'm not worried, but growing impatient. Why do you make me wait? Again and again? But I wait. Late is better than never. We have all night and all tomorrow. I try sleeping. It works for a few minutes at a time. Six-forty-five. Where are you, Julia? Seven o'clock. I should go meet you. But we'll get hung up at your apartment and never get out to my place. I sleep again. Seven-twenty. I'm through waiting.

Some vague thoughts go through my mind. I suspect there's a drinking problem, but I'm experiencing denial. I refuse to think, consciously, that there *is* a drinking problem. That could ruin everything. Somehow we'll work through it, *when* it surfaces. (Roy, ex-husband, big, teddy bear-like, heart of gold, tells me later, "It *would* have surfaced.")

And it has. Our very first time together alone. A ride in the country. I show you a piece of land I'm hoping to buy. But what is a twelve-pack of beer doing on the floor of "Little Blue"? (what we had named her car). I don't mention the beer and you don't offer. And the first time you visit my home, beer is on your breath, slightly, your speech is slurred, slightly, you're not perfectly steady on your feet. But I don't mention it. I deny it. And the third time. Laura is with us. You're showing me a place in the country where you had lived. You tell me bulldozing is planned. You're unhappy. I don't blame you. For the first time your personality has changed, at times almost caustic to me. Again I deny the possible reason.

The fourth and last time. Saturday, July 12, about eleven PM. You're carrying one bottle of beer from the car. I stop you. I don't keep alcohol of any kind in my house. So, you can't either. It's our first really unpleasant moments. Julia sits on the step in the mosquitoes. Laura stays with her. I go inside. In moments they come in. Julia opens the bottle and pours the beer down the drain, "That's it," she says.

So I don't think about Julia's possible drinking problem. I choose to believe she has made a first step in conquering it. And I don't worry.

****

But enough time has passed. I'll go home and wait for her there. She'll come to the parking lot, find out that I won't, always, wait for her, she'll follow me home, we'll hug, we'll talk, and that will be that. Everything will be OK again.

I won't always wait for you, Julia. You have to learn that and straighten up a little bit.

But even with these self-righteous and self-serving thoughts, I am, subconsciously, worried. And a late-day cloudy sky doesn't help. Where are you, Julia? Why didn't you come?

So I go home, put my feet up, and will wait.

I'm not worried.

I'm downhearted, though...and worried too, subconsciously. I had waited like this—asleep in a recliner—once before. And at eleven PM they come. I am awakened by cuddling, Julia on one side, Laura the other. What a wonderful awakening. That's what will happen this time.

But this time, subconsciously, I'm worried.

Sleep comes.

And Julia comes to me. But it's different. She's above me...we do not speak...it's, not, *exactly,* a dream…sleep returns. I don't know how much time passes, probably minutes, or even just seconds. Suddenly I'm wide awake. It's totally pitch dark. I'm not even sure where I am. I struggle to find a light switch. It's eleven PM. Julia, were you here? Did I not wake up to your loving and you left again, with a broken heart? What? Where *are* you, Julia?

It has rained. I go outside with a flashlight. If she was here there will be tire tracks. I walk clear out to the street. There are no tire tracks. Nothing. She's mad at me for not waiting. She didn't come to me. But she was here! I *saw* her!

I saw you, Julia. Was it a dream? Was it your spirit? Saying goodbye? Saying you were sorry for being late? Again? And why so late in the night? (But, eleven PM, your usual time for arriving.) But you had to have passed hours earlier—how long does it take to get into heaven, anyway? Was there a long line? Tons of paperwork? What? So many unanswered questions. We left here on earth can never know the answers. We can never understand "Why?" We can only accept. Downhearted and disturbed I return inside.

She didn't come.

We're having our first fight. I'm being stubborn, she's being stubborn, and we're ruining our time off together.

****

The next morning I'm still not, consciously, worried.

The telephone repair man comes. He complains about my mosquitoes. I nearly bite his head off. This is not me to act this way. We both apologize and he quickly fixes my phone.

Maybe I *am* worried.

This day, Monday, July 14, our day off, I mow my lawn, run the weed-whacker, do some rearranging and cleaning in both houses (Julia was supposed to be helping), and watch for Little Blue to appear in my driveway. I'm preparing my yard, my home, my life, to receive Julia and Laura. I've talked to the school principal, called prospective local babysitters, talked to the postmaster about two new names coming to my post office box number. Even though we're having a silence-fight I will continue preparing for them to arrive with bag and baggage. Winter is soon coming. We've talked about it again and again. We're planning a life together. The three of us. I've got to be ready for them. We're becoming a family. If one goes somewhere we all three go. We're bonding. Once I needed to trim my moustache. The downstairs bathroom is full of women. I say I'll go upstairs. "I want to watch," Laura says, and follows. "I want to watch too," Julia says, and follows too. But the light was better downstairs. But, anywhere for a family affair.

But Little Blue does not arrive.

Well, we'll see each other at work tomorrow and we'll work this "fight" out. Everything will be OK.

By five o'clock I'm approaching devastated. Julia would not make me wait this long. She would have broken the silence. I should have. My phone works again. No answer. Julia's phone rings and rings. And she doesn't have her answering machine on. But she's forgotten before. I don't worry—But I *am* worried.

I'll sleep. I do sleep.

Then comes the call from babysitter and best friend, Holly, "Where's Julia?"

I don't know. *Now*, I'm worried.

Holly and I arrive at Julia's apartment about the same time. Nobody there. Holly will keep Laura. I will retrace some of our past tracks. I'll check the Fargo airport. We loved watching the planes together. Julia shared her dream of being a pilot. My old Chevy burns the road. Then I see Little Blue sitting in a field. A terrible foreboding strikes me. The brakes squeal as I slam my foot. I pull onto an approach to go back. A car coming from each direction makes me wait, seemingly a long time—What's the matter with them?! *CAN'T THEY SEE I HAVE TO GET TO MY JULIA?!*

The old Chevy squeals again as I finally get back to the road. I park on the approach. Little Blue's tire tracks lead nearly straight into the field, as if Julia, purposely, has driven there—WHY?! No footprints lead from the car. She's inside. She has to be. The field is muddy. Water has filled the tire tracks. She has to be inside—She *can't* be!—that might mean....

Adrenaline, fear, disbelief, all grip me as I hurry toward the driver side, straining to see into the window, knowing what I'll see, denying what I know I'll see—*SHE CAN'T BE THERE!*

But she is there. Lying over in the seat as if just sleeping. But I know she's not just sleeping, but I'll keep denying it until—

I throw the door open, touch and hold her upper arm as I have touched her hundreds of times before...oh, Julia, what happened?

I hold her arm for a long time. Her skin is hot from the sun but there is no internal fire. She's gone. She was on her way to meet me, and on time. I should have waited for her. I should have gone looking for her. I should have been WORRIED!

I did none of those things. Instead I got impatient and went home.

911 soon brought the police and an ambulance. For awhile I wasn't allowed to leave. I suppose, under the circumstances, there is always the possibility of fowl play. An autopsy would later say an aortic aneurysm caused Julia's death, that her only hope would have been that she was already on the operating table when the attack came.

****

Three weeks have passed. I still have not cried, openly. When my father died I cried, while my nephew, Robert, and then my niece, Debbie, held me. But that crying helped release me. I came to accept his death, and be happy for him going to his eternal reward.

When I'm alone tears for Julia well first in my stomach, then my throat. Sometimes they escape. A few. Not really for you, Julia. I am happy you've gotten your reward for putting in your time on earth. No, the tears are not for you, but for me, and for little Laura. We miss you so. And I'm alone again. But not alone. Your two other lovely daughters have welcomed me into their lives. But still, I can allow myself to intrude in their lives just so often.

****

Julia, you and I met fifteen months ago. I remember well. You faced me, gave me one smile, shook my hand, said "Hello," and that was about the last word you said to me that I truly heard and understood. You never initiated conversation. You rarely went on break with the rest of us ("I don't work hard enough," you would say.) You were so quiet, and shy, soft-spoken, ("You want to hear my drill sergeant voice?"). But, if you would never initiate conversation then neither would I. And I wasn't exactly eager to try reaching further into someone's life either. Obviously, neither of us was very interested in reaching out. So we didn't. Our first months were spent with barely eye-contact. But even then something did connect. But even so, when the night shift began I grabbed it, then saw you only briefly in the distance, and not every day. If you won't talk to me, well, what's the point of me trying to talk to you?

Until the last morning that season. About 5am. My last night. For some reason unknown to me, Julia, you have moved to the late night shift. "The birds were singing," you had since reminded me. Yes, I remember...but what were you even doing there, let alone be on break with me? I had questioned whether you even liked me. But you were there. Just the two of us. Alone together for the first time.

I was telling you of my father's death just two months earlier, how hard it had been on me, and how thankful I had been to have a job to come to or I didn't know if I could have survived. I don't remember you saying anything. You just listened. Your full attention, to me.

The shift ends. We shake hands again and part. To my knowledge nothing has happened between us. But at least we talked. That is, I talked. You listened. You always listened to me, as if I was saying something important.

Months pass. The 1997 manufacturing season approaches. I wonder if she'll be there?

She is.

We're glad to see each other.

This time at our work station I place myself across from you, so that both my ears face you and I can hear you. We begin talking. And talk some more. Then a lot more. Then there's a phone call.

And then another. Then another and another. Then we're seeing each other after work. We explore the countryside, thrill to skydivers landing in the sun and plan our own jump, watch planes coming and going, walk the Sheyenne and Red Rivers, toss the Frisbee, go once to my church and plan Sunday School for Laura, set off a 400-string of firecrackers in the middle of main street of my home town at two in the morning, then laugh about it and hug and skedaddle, and we share music and coffee and talk, and talk, and talk...and begin falling in love, and finally the romantic Moody Blues concert. My nephews and their wives way down on the floor said we "looked pretty cozy up there." Yes, Julia and I ignore the multitudes of people and are cozy. We make first love this night, then share breakfast (one toast, a little juice, coffee), first of many. Love for Julia came so easily.

Then comes Laura. Six years of raw energy and perfect charm. Laura comes to like me immediately. Julia says, "It's because she knows I'm happy."

Then comes Alana. Just graduated from high school, buoyant, smart, anticipating life, 18 but still too young to lose her mother.

Luke, who endears me with "Crazy Jim".

And Celeste, who I yet had not met and who would soon marry Luke. But she opens her arms, is warm, strong. She becomes my strength to face this unbelievable grief.

For my Julia, my beloved who loved me, who loved everything I did and couldn't do enough for me, who opened me to love, again, has fallen.

Time has stopped. What was important no longer is. We were together, closely, for such a short time, that sometimes it's as if our love never happened. But it did happen.

The funeral day arrives. We all grieve for our loss. I meet Julia's amiable brother, Kent, "She called me her Chuck Norris," he says. "Her hero." Was I a hero to Julia? I hope so. She was to me. That night we, her family, "release her spirit to heaven" with dozens of helium-filled balloons, and set off fireworks.

But who is this man, her family must wonder? Who is this stranger? Yes, I'm nearly a stranger. But Julia knew me, knew everything about me and loved me for

it, and made me love her for loving me. And Laura knows me. For that short time

the three of us became one.

But Julia and Laura are no longer coming to my home and into my life. Right now almost nothing matters anymore. Home is a place of loneliness and despair. Driving to and from work is a time of remembering sorrow—yes, good times too, but mostly sorrow—it took me twenty years to find Julia. Only at work does my mind sometimes release me.

And Laura. Laura matters. She maybe soon would have become my step-daughter. Now she talks to me as Julia once did. We talk of many things on our days together while we shop, explore YUNKER FARM, CHUCK E CHEESE, city parks and playgrounds...she asks once, "Jim, what do you think of when you're alone?" and often brings up "Mom," mainly, "Jim, do you miss Mom right now?" Yes, Laura, I miss Mom. Do you?

"Yes."

But, Julia, I don't know what to do with my love for little Laura. I came to love her because she is a part of you. It was a natural, easy thing to do. I can't turn that love off just because you're gone. With this child I feel a bonding that never came from my ten nieces and nephews, nor from my fifteen great nieces and nephews. It's different, much deeper. In her little arms, in her tight hugs that I need so much, I feel loved, wanted, important, just as I felt from you, Julia. But she now, *suddenly*, has so many more people in her life. Any person, even a little girl, has just so much room in her heart for love. Two loving sisters. Several father figures. Babysitters. A possible future foster family.

And there's her natural father. Laura is a special child who needs patience, understanding, above all true and dependable love. But from my one meeting with him I find it hard to believe that he would provide what Laura needs.

So is there room for me? *Should* there be room for me? Or does my presence just make Laura's loss worse for her? And when the possible foster family does arrive, Laura will have to make yet another adjustment. Should I gracefully offer to bow out? For Laura's sake? So that the transition maybe will be smoother? I don't know. Others will have to help me with this decision. Each time I come to see her I fear being forgotten. No, she won't forget me. But what about rejection? I was just her mother's boyfriend, and for a very short time. Yes, we were planning a life together, the three of us, but events did not move fast enough. Our life together did not happen.

And then time ended.

Julia, I spent a week writing this letter to you. I thought it would make me feel better. It has, some. But I still miss you, and I guess I always will. You filled me so completely with your love, and now I feel so empty....

Theologians say God has a reason for everything He does. Philosophers say things are happening as they are meant to happen. But all I know for sure is that Laura and me both lost you, Julia, the one we loved the most.

With all my love, Jimmy….

****

Eventually, Julia's three daughters and I have drifted apart. I think about them and I care about them, but I don't *know* about them. Celeste married Luke and they have two sons and a daughter. Alana also got married and has a family. Laura ended up staying with Celeste. I'm glad about that. Staying with her big sister was best. Laura is eighteen years old and a senior in high school this year, 2009. I wonder about her, I care about her, and sometimes I even worry about her….

I wish you all the best in life, Laura, love, Jim

****

The old Chevy I mentioned earlier was my dad's last car, a 1971 Chevrolet Impala that I drove until 2006. Dad told me, "Jim, this is my last car." It lasted me ten more years after he died. I wish I would have had a place to store it. It required repairs occasionally, but it never quit. It just started taking too much gas. (And, no, I don't still have it.)

12

YOKOSUKA

Before leaving for Westpac there is one more major training session, for everybody. I've been hearing about it and it doesn't sound pretty. It has to do with swimming. Not exactly swimming but it does take place in the water. *Under* water. I've noticed this 150 foot tower. It reminds me of a small town water tower only the tank is the same diameter top to bottom. Training will include a pressure test, one of the things I missed by not going to sub school. Just the sound of the word 'pressure' is unsettling.

Early in the morning, with towels and swim trunks, we all walk over there. It's a sunny day, as is usual at Pearl Harbor. I mean, in Hawaii, it can be raining sometimes and you just walk in it. You don't care that you're getting wet—well, unless it's *pouring*. Maybe you don't care because you know the sun will be out very soon and you will quickly dry out again. The tank in the distance looks ominous. We've already received training with the Steinke hoods. Steinke is the name of the guy who developed the hood, a new type of life jacket for escaping from a sunken submarine.

In both the Forward and After Torpedo Rooms the hatches leading topside are modified for escape. In the forward room just the hatch area itself is modified. It's big enough for three to five men to get into at once and stand. Then the side watertight door would be closed, then it's flooded with sea water and equalized with sea pressure, then the top hatch is opened, pressurized air would fill the life jackets, and, one at a time we would climb the short ladder and float to the surface. In the After Torpedo Room the entire compartment would be flooded and a lot more men could get out a lot more quickly. Only it wouldn't be quite as easy as it may have sounded.

First we would have to be sunken in water shallow enough so that this would work. The tank is 150 feet, so they must think that we could get out from that depth or even deeper, but still, it would have to be shallow *enough*. But no matter how deep—if the hull hadn't yet collapsed—wouldn't we at least want to try? I think so.

Second, we would hope a radio message got out (or could be gotten out) that we were in trouble, so that when we got to the surface there would be rescue vessels waiting, or at least on their way. I mean no use getting to the surface just to die of exposure, or from sharks. Right?

It's one of those contingencies that must be planned for, and then trained for. Navy divers will train us and ensure we all survive training.

We receive about an hour of classroom training, then get into our swim trunks, ride in small groups to the fifty-foot level (that's fifty feet from the top.) Then we get into this small place (like an old-fashioned hotel elevator), and that compartment will be flooded and pressurized. The sound is like that when Reeves is blowing Bow Buoyancy. A real blast!

I clamp my fingers over my nose and blow out. My ears pop. The blast of air continues. I keep popping my ears and swallowing. Flooded, pressurized, equalized. My head feels like...it's hard to describe, maybe like listening to calm air whistling through an empty sea shell, only real loud, or like I had just taken five hundred puffs of a cigarette and all at once, but I'm not exactly dizzy, just feeling really, really, high. The hatch is opened. One at a time we go. My turn comes. I slip the hood over my head. Breathe normally. Right. I feel the pressurized air filling my life jacket and the hood surrounding my head. The air stops. I feel a pat on my shoulder. Time to go. I grasp the top of the hatch, duck my head, and step into the mockup ocean. Fifty feet of water above me, one hundred below. Next, turn and face the hatch, stand at attention, then let go.

All very quickly because that life jacket *really* wants to quickly take me to the surface. Now comes the hard part. Imagine breathing this compressed air. As one rises toward the surface, toward less pressure, that compressed air is going to expand. You must get rid of it or your lungs will explode. (In the classroom, the possibility of that happening kind of bothered me.) And that part of our classroom training was very, very, clear to me, that I had to do it…correctly.

And there is a way to get rid of that air. I shout, "Ho! Ho! Ho!" grab a shallow breath, "Ho! Ho! Ho!" shallow breath, "Ho! Ho! Ho!" Imagine this. Your lungs already feel like they're out of air. *Way* out—But they're not. But they *feel* that way. I don't know how many "Ho, ho, hos," I get out, before I feel myself grabbed and pulled into another small compartment part of the way up. Evidently I wasn't "Ho, ho, hoing!" enough. The Navy diver who pulls me out (likely saving my life) has a black crewcut and big expressive eyes. He reminds me of EARNEST BORGNINE. He's a hero.

I didn't exactly pass that training, but I did receive the training. So if Carbonero sinks in salvageable water I will have an idea of what to do. Another one of those things I won't spend too much time thinking, or worrying, about.

****

World War II type diesel submarines are small. Compared to most other ocean going vessels they are like a cork in a barrel. In heavy, stormy seas we must ride the waves. No diving. We could dive but there is a problem surfacing. At some point during surfacing, the point of balance becomes close to zero, zero gravity, and a well-placed crash of a broadside wave could capsize us. So in stormy seas we must stay on the surface. But if we're going somewhere that's OK because there's not much speed while submerged. About eight knots. Faster if we're snorkeling. But a major drain on the batteries no matter what.

Whereas, with four engines running on the surface at standard speed we can reach about nineteen knots. A knot is a little further than a mile. One nautical mile equals

about 1.15 statute miles. So nineteen knots are about 21.8 miles per hour (but not nearly that fast when the sea is really rough.) Imagine crossing the Pacific Ocean at that speed. Plenty of time for reading, playing cards, sleeping, writing letters home.

And for standing watches. Lookout has become my favorite job. We're on our way to Yokosuka, Japan, about 30 miles south of Tokyo, with Yokohama in between. It sits on latitude 35.18, about the same as Amarillo, Texas, and Memphis, Tennessee. We're heading dead into the waves. A really, really, *really*, huge one is coming. It's gray, and reminds me of the sandhills back home, and the tidal wave in the movie POISIDEN ADVENTURE. It keeps coming, steam-rolling, in fact. It's going to hit hard. We plough into a slightly smaller wave first. The bow noses in and goes down...and stays down. The big one is boiling toward us. The bow is still down. That wave is going to bury us. It must be sixty feet high. No, maybe forty—whatever, it's way, way higher than our heads—Jesus!

Here we go again with that zero point of balance. For every dive the bow takes it must also rise again to face the next wave. The bow is not rising. It can't. Too much water. The huge wave continues its journey toward us. I look around. The other lookout glances back at me. His eyes look how mine feel: Wide open and unblinking. Nobody says anything. The OOD is staunch, facing toward that monster bearing down on us, covering all sign of the deck and superstructure.

Finally from the OOD and spoken basically calmly: "Hang on!"

Well, we weren't exactly not hanging on, and we are lashed in, and we are wearing foul weather gear...but the idea of what that wave is going to do to us...

Above the crashing of the waves comes a sound that I can only describe as a board bending, fibers stretching and snapping, the sound just before stress breaks that board. But this boat is made of steel, and it's the stress of steel making this sound.

Is this mutherfucker going to break?

But just when all looks lost, the bow—that zero point of gravity that physics says it must do—rises and breaks the surface. The monster wave still smacks us hard and for what seems like a long, long, time (likely 4-5 seconds) appears to bury everything. Quite a lot of water even pours down the Conning Tower hatch.

But we survive. I look over at the other lookout. Water is pouring off his cap and coat too. We both grin. Even the OOD glances back and grins. After all, he's human too; he's in the Navy for this adventure too, like us, for this thrilling ride across uncharted seas.

Uncharted? How can I say that? But I can say that. Have you ever seen the ocean? Do you see any tracks across it? Any signs or highways? Of course not. So each person's trek across it is like the first time. Each voyage a new discovery.

The only signs on the ocean are crossroads on maps and charts. Coordinates, where invisible lines of longitude cross invisible lines of latitude. Crossroads and coordinates that are checked daily and constantly with the gyro compass and manually with the sextant. By day with the sun's location in the sky at a certain time of day and time of year. By night with the stars. The Captain, the other officers and the quartermasters know where we are. That's their job. I don't worry about it. I'm here for the adventure.

And for my specific job of firing torpedoes. If necessary. It never becomes necessary to fire in, as they say, anger. But we fire exercise shots. Torpedoes with dummy warheads. The Mark 16, a twenty-foot-long steam torpedo from World War II. In 1963 we still carry them. They're the old warhorses but they pack a wallop. 500 pounds of TNT. I fire just one. An exercise shot with the warhead filled with sea water, and a gyro compass that gets just one setting. Not coordinates, just a heading. Like a gun firing a bullet. It goes out the tube and turns to its heading and then goes hell bent for election to its target, or not.

I'm in the After Torpedo Room, where we live with torpedoes, and sleep with them, on top of them, beside them. Mostly live ones fully loaded with their TNT just lacking their primers (detonators). But the detonators are on board too, just not in the same compartment with the torpedoes, least not in peacetime. I stand at tube #4. My hand is on the pull-plunger that will fire the torpedo with compressed air. Chief Ickes, my boss, is here. (Chief Ickes literally kicked me in the ass one time when I was royally fucking up. That was embarrassing, Chief, but I really liked you. Thanks for straightening me out that day.) And Lynchwick and Abare are here, and Larry Lagle and Jesse Dasher, and Jerry Kochert, Fire Control Technician. We all have our jobs.

The order comes, "Flood Tube #4."

"Open the outer door."

Then the final order, "Fire!"

I pull the plunger.

WHOOSH! Only a hundred times louder.

The whole submarine shudders as the steam fish leaves the boat, makes its one turn, then rushes with a single propeller up to forty knots to its target. The exercise explosion is an internal blast of air that blows the sea water from the head and the Mark 16 floats harmlessly to the surface. It will be picked up by the surface ship that today was our target.

****

We arrive at Yokosuka. I'm qualified now. I have my dolphins. I can go ashore anytime I want. In the submarine Navy we have no regular paydays. But every time we arrive in port, whether we've been out ten days or six weeks, there is a paycheck waiting. The smart sailors, the ones who have been around for awhile and others who are just plain smart, will make their pay last for their entire time in port, and beyond. Others, the dumb ones, will spend it all the first night.

Unfortunately, I usually fall into the latter category.

I go ashore in full dress blue uniform with several of my shipmates. The drinks flow. The music plays. We dance, we sing, we find a girl.

One with curly hair that doesn't quite reach her shoulders finds me. She's round, she's pretty, she's Japanese, "What you name, saila?"

It's my first exposure to a foreign national. I answer plainly, "Nelly."

"Newlry?"

I swear there's an "L" sound in there but the "R" is strongest. "Yes."

"I am glad to meet you, Newlry-san. I am Kimiko-san."

I'm in love. And I will fall in love again and again and again, with every Japanese, Chinese, Philippino, girl I meet in the next three years during two Westpac cruises that include stops at four Japanese cities, besides Yokosuka, Sasebo, Yokohoma, and Tokyo.

They warned us about her next question: "What ship you on?"

"Carbonero." That question we could answer.

"What ship numba?" That question we couldn't answer.

Even around Pearl Harbor the Pacific has what's referred to as Russian trawlers. The name suggests fishing boat. The Navy suggests electronics surveillance boat. Before leaving for Westpac we had painted over the ship's number. The closer we get to Asia, to Asiatic Soviet Russia, the more will regular Soviet Navy ships be about. No use making identification of our ship easy. But every new woman I meet will ask the same question, and sometimes the same woman will ask the same question every time I see her. If they aren't spies for, someone, then why would they all ask that question: "What ship numba?"

And why did they want to know?

What possible difference could it make?

We spend a few days in Hong Kong too. There I buy a custom made, reversible vest, custom made boots, a dress white sharkskin uniform, and fall in love just once. I don't remember her name (maybe she didn't even tell me.) I remember a movie about Hong Kong. I think the late WILLIAM HOLDEN was the main actor.

SUSIE WONG was either the main actress or the main female character, or maybe the name of the movie. In the movie there is a steep hill, where the worst slums are located, nothing but huts and soil. In the movie it rains, and that hill literally melts. I maybe didn't see the actual hill from the movie, but I saw plenty of slums and hills that I could easily imagine melting in the rain.

One of the Chinese tailors invites a group of us to a fancy meal. Unfortunately, a lot of the food did not appeal to me but the meal must have been memorable or why would I remember it?

Food is one of my excuses for not volunteering for Vietnam. Also, I heard one guy tell what he had heard from another guy. A lot of hearsay there, but most likely true: "He just went nuts and kept shooting the guy long after he was dead!" I can believe that is nearly exactly how it would happen. Anyway, in 1966, a few months before I am scheduled to get out, a notice appears on the bulletin board: Wanted: Volunteers for shore duty in Vietnam. Well, I considered it. I asked around. It meant a lot more training for one thing, including a prisoner-of-war camp with marine guards, and being required to eat what some would call garbage for food. So food became my main excuse for not volunteering. I'm pretty sure I could eat garbage if that's all I had, in order to actually survive. But to eat it in training, no, I wouldn't do it.

And there were other reasons: Since I had less than a year left it meant extending my enlistment (and I had already done that, which I haven't gotten to yet); then there's the final reason, the one I'm not proud of: The idea of going to Vietnam, likely seeing combat, scared me. Those last words were not easy to write. Over fifty thousand of my brothers were killed in Vietnam and I was afraid to go. The closest I got to Vietnam was on the ocean. How close I don't know, it seemed like maybe two miles, maybe more, because I could clearly see jungle and waterfalls. It appeared to be a very beautiful place. I don't understand how anything bad could have been happening there. How wrong I was.

****

I knew that sooner or later I would have to make that admission. Having done it I don't feel any better, no weight has left my shoulders. But also, I feel, in my own tiny way, by making that admission, I am honoring those who *did* go. My best friend, James Rockstad, joined the marines and *did* go, and he came home alive. Another good friend, Dennis Herrick, Air Force, spent his time in Thailand, typing "Trail Watcher" intelligence reports (24/7) that helped plan and initiate bombing runs on the Ho Chi Minh Trail; he also came home alive. John King, Army Spec-4 mechanic, worked on heavy equipment near Ban Kruat, Thailand, next door to a US Air Force base, and near Cambodia (today Kampuchea). John, a good friend clear back to Sunday School, came home alive too, married Sue and returned to farming. Rick Fowler, another good friend from Sunday School, Sergeant, Artillery, 12th Marines, top secret clearance, was stationed near Dong Ha and the DMZ. They were surrounded by a mine field; even so, the enemy "…still managed to get close enough to fire rocket-propelled grenades at us…every night." Three things Rick said really stuck with me, as they have with him: One, the Vietnamese people, the peasants; their lives amounted only to Survival. Second, upon arrival it was a long, *vulnerable*, time before he was issued a weapon. (Later in the war soldiers arrived battle-ready…go figure….) And the third thing was seeing rows of black body bags filled and waiting for transport. Rick came home alive, eventually married Debbie and began trucking. I said all these friends came home alive, but were they still the same young and impressionable boys who entered the armed forces? I think not.

Still another good friend, Jerome Ellenson, Army Sergeant, paid the ultimate price. When the TRAVELING WALL came to Moorhead, Minnesota, I went, and I found Jerome's name. In school I called him Jerry. Jerry was a good and kind man.

****

One more bit about Vietnam. After the war was long over I did meet one guy who shared his experience. He told about this little kid running at him with what he assumed was a live grenade, so, yes, he shot him. Did he do right? Or should he have waited till the kid got to him so he could have *checked* the grenade? And therefore probably got both of them killed. No, he did right by shooting first. Sure, the kid was probably innocent; the kid didn't come up with the idea of running at an American soldier with a live grenade on his own. There are probably hundreds of stories like this, and 99% of the soldiers were likely correct in their actions...but that created the name of "babykillers", and that unfortunate term preceded them home.

****

As I said, I don't feel any better but I will go on telling my own story.

Also in Hong Kong they told us not to ride the rickshaws (a two-wheeled cart pulled by a coolie). That's like a mother telling her six-year-old son to stay out of the chocolate-chip cookie jar. I hail a rickshaw (just like hailing a cab.) He stops. I climb aboard. I instruct him to take me to wherever it was American sailors went to get their US dollars changed into Hong Kong dollars. He tells me what the fare will be.

When he goes past the front entrance I remind him but I don't get too excited. I suppose I could have jumped out. We pass through an alley and arrive in back of the building, among about a dozen other coolies and rickshaws. Suddenly the fare triples. I protest. But I'm surrounded by several grim-faced Chinese men. There is a surge toward me. I hand my coolie driver his triple fare and consider myself having gotten off lucky.

Had I reported this driver he wouldn't have gone to jail. Hong Kong jails are full. I witnessed Hong Kong police punish wrongdoers with canes right on the street. This driver likely would have thought a cane beating to be worth his triple fare.

In the Philippine Islands we visit Manila and Olongapo. The taxis are like open-air, fifties station wagons with banners. There I meet Mercy. She gives me a picture and signs it, "Lest you forget."

I didn't forget you, Mercy.

But, alas, most of the women I meet during my four years in the Navy I do forget. I try to treat them all like ladies, but I do forget most of them.

Maybe that sounds like I don't respect women. I do. I respect women and I love women, and I really respect women's rights, *and* their right to choose. I'm talking about abortion. I hate the thought of abortion, and I'm sure most (maybe all) women do too, but there are times.... Back in the eighties I volunteered as an escort at the Women's Health Clinic in Fargo (when they were located just off Main, I think.) I don't remember the exact years, or days, and I didn't keep a diary, but I remember well the happenings, mainly that we were two groups of people, standing at opposite ends of the "rights" spectrum, literally, and we at times faced each other from just a few feet apart. We also played IMAGINE, by JOHN LENNON, loudly, at times.

Sometimes we on our side even held hands, or maybe wrists (just hands could have been easily broken through) and sometimes things became that tense that we had to actually plan to hold our ground. There was one guy on their side who was so huge that he could have squashed any three of the people on our side, and a few times he did take a run at us. We always tightened our lines and braced but he never came all the way. Thank goodness. Because there would have been damage done. To us. I don't know if he was being directed to do as he did or if he was doing it all on his own thinking. Somehow I don't think he was capable of too much actual planning on his own, and was there just for scare tactics.

I met a girl there who I had at one time worked with. She was surprised to see me, that I would be active to support women's rights. So I told her yes, I do support women's rights, but that I also was there making a statement of my own (I guess mainly just to myself) against all radical groups who are trying to take away law-abiding citizens' rights to choose...whatever...and then I mentioned gun-owners-rights. Her shocked look made me think that she thought that I had just asked her for sex, or something.

Maybe I was wrong to include *other* rights; at least I shouldn't probably have verbalized that to anyone. For certain not to her. And I didn't mean to get political in my autobiography; (I meant this to be entertaining, not political.) I maybe will get attacked for my standing, but the subject, sort of, came up.

Later, when I was leaving on one of those days, I discover that I had locked my keys in my vehicle, and who should come by but one of the leaders from the other side. He helped me get into my vehicle all right, and with what? A clothes hanger.

Maybe everyone won't see the irony here but some of you will.

Today, June 10, 2009, it is reported in THE FORUM that the clinic that the murdered Doctor George Tiller, Kansas, ran "...will be permanently closed, his family said Tuesday..." So it appears the anti-abortion people are winning, if all they have to do is murder the person in charge of a women's health clinic.

****

Returning to the far past, there was one girl I met at Yokosuka—and I can't remember the name of the place but it's where they give hot baths and massages. Her name was Mariko-san. She wasn't a Geisha Girl but she looked and acted how—in my mind—I think one probably would look and act. But true Geisha Girls were out-of-this-world expensive—so I had heard—so, no, she wasn't a Geisha Girl. But I think she *could* have been. (I still don't know, exactly, what it is that a Geisha Girl does. I can only imagine that they treat men way beyond how many/most men deserve to be treated.)

Anyway, Mariko-san gives me my first hot bath and massage. I'm a little shy about getting undressed, without doing...well, you know. (Anyway, *she's* not undressed, so why do I have to get undressed?) So, I get undressed, and I don't remember which was first, the steam bath or the hot bath? What I *do* remember: The hot bath, to me, seemed to be *excruciatingly* hot, and the steam bath brought on a definite claustrophobic feeling when she closed those doors that could only be opened from the outside. (Seems to me James Bond got trapped in one of those things, and, it also seems to me that he got out, and on his own, but *he* was James Bond.)

But, Mariko-san eventually opened the doors and let me out again, and then I think, came the hot bath. She washed me. I remember at one point her giving me the rag and soap...she didn't speak English but did get the message across that I was to wash my private parts myself. I remember her smiling about that, even laughing in her gentle Geisha-like way. Next came the massage. I got down on my stomach, she put a towel over my middle, and then massaged nearly every square inch of my body, and my soul.

I've thought of part of the name of that place: Palace: *Something…* Palace. After the first time, *Something…*Palace became one of my favorite places. Every time we came back into port, during our six-month Westpac cruise, my first stop would be *Something…*Palace, where I always asked for Mariko-san. If she wasn't there I went without a hot bath. I even asked Mariko-san to walk on my back once. I knew masseuses sometimes did that, and how heavy could this tiny Japanese girl be, anyway? The answer: Heavy. I thought that tiny girl was going to squash me, and she giggled about it, too. I only asked her to do it that one time. We developed a special relationship. I came to adore Mariko-san, and, no, we never…did it.

I've met and been with other American girls too. Three stand out, but of course I won't name them and destroy their privacy. One was married, one was divorced (that lasted three years and then I was divorced—how about that? Divorced but never married.) and the one single one made me absolutely crazy, and not in a good way. I won't describe her. I will say she took me on my first trip with marijuana. (I took only two trips; the second one was happy, more like an alcohol drunk.) She was driving her vehicle. I was a willing to unwilling passenger. Mainly I looked out the window at the world going by one second at about eight mph, the next second at eighty mph, up and down, but I doubt either speed was very accurate. The important thing was her face: One second angelic, the next demonic, and that's how she was when we were sober, too. I am so lucky I didn't stay involved with her. Nevertheless it was a failed romance, one I invested full heart in. All three of them, but sometimes things just aren't meant to be.

To finish this section, at Midway Island we meet the goony birds (albatrosses), and their young. This is their mating and molting season. They can't fly for us. We don't get to see them crash land.

****

Looking back I sometimes wonder just what kind of a blockhead was I? For instance I rarely asked questions like, where are we? What are we doing? Usually, sooner or later I would hear from the grapevine where we were, what we were doing. I guess I always assumed somebody would always tell me where we were and what we were doing. Or anything else I actually *needed* to know.

We get so far north one time that there is ice on the sail. I never expected it to be this cold on the Pacific. I guess I thought the whole Pacific was tropical. I don't know how I reached that conclusion. We're operating off South Korea. We have a squad of South Korean Marines on board in the Forward Torpedo Room. (And they are all really tough-looking customers: Really, definitely, Military.) Somewhere offshore we will come to "All Stop". They will take their weapons and rafts topside. We will partially submerge. And they will launch and play their war game. But is this a game? Or something else?

The Cold War occasionally gets a little hot around Korea. Maybe this South Korean Marine launch is not a game at all. Nobody tells me and I don't ask. So now, over forty years later, I'm still wondering. What the hell were we doing there? And what the hell was the name of that Korean port where we pulled in after dark and left before day break? Probably was lucky for me that I had duty that night and couldn't go ashore. It would have been real, real easy to get into trouble in the few hours we were there. Why? Because a blockhead feels he has to do every *thing*, every time.

****

Back to my first night in Yokosuka. Kimiko-san and I have retired to a hotel room. My virginity leaves me. There are no bells or banners, barely a memory. I want love. I have always wanted love, a wife, a family, not this prostituted sex. This is not looking back forty years and thinking how I *should* have thought then. This is how I *thought* then. It's how I've always thought. I've always wanted just one woman to love. On a different note, the idea of marriage, the possibility of being *trapped* with the wrong woman, kind of scares me, and the idea of going through a soul-wringing divorce also scares me. I've seen divorce happen to three women close to me; it's not life's happiest time. Anyway….

Even so, my experiences in the Orient taught me about life.

****

You remember I said there were two times in my naval career when I felt violent toward another shipmate? The second time happens at a ship's party. A ship's party is one of those occasions when everybody goes except the skeleton crew on duty. It's an event that calls for renting a whole hotel or at least a big part of one and is definitely planned for: Food, booze, women.

One of the officers has stolen my woman, Ruby-san, my lady of the night for the evening. As usual I am in love with her, and I am drunk. So my drunken love requires me to put my fist through a glass door. Lots of blood later I'm bandaged and passed out. When I wake up (to a cheer no less) and when what happens, happens, I'm already pissed so it doesn't take much to get me there.

But to get there I have to go still further back. Boat sailors living on World War II diesel submarines are required to sleep under quite crowded conditions. I mean in the After Battery the bunks can be piled four high and a man six and a half feet tall cannot even stand comfortably upright. Being a torpedoman's mate I got to sleep in the After Torpedo room. My main bunkmates were the overhead in my face, a mark 16 steam torpedo below me and the stern planes motor beside me. To get to my bunk I had to play Tarzan. But I had privacy.

Boat sailors also go to sea for extended periods of time. We read, we play cards and board games like Acey-Deucey, cribbage, chess, we sleep, and we talk.

Before I got my high swinging bunk in the overhead I slept six inches from the floor on a bunk that swung down. A card game could easily go on right beside me, and often did. We were somewhere hot and sweaty. Laying under the blankets, or even a sheet, was not an option. But I should have been.

Back then I had barely gotten the word "homosexual" introduced to me. About all I knew is that it was guys liking guys. (And I hadn't even imagined yet that girls liked girls too. What a pleasant surprise *that* was.) Were there any homosexuals on the Carbonero? I don't know. I doubt it. I liked women so I didn't spend any time thinking and wondering about homosexuals and what they did. But the talk and joking was sometimes rampant.

Anyway, there was a game of poker going on right beside me. I was sound asleep, so I don't know *exactly* what happened. But I heard about it. Boy, did I hear about it. Everybody on board eventually heard about it, and talked about it.

Evidently I was having a good dream. You know the kind, about ladies, the kind that can lead to a wet dream. And, evidently, my penis found its way out of my skivvies. You know, a sort of semi-erection. And, evidently, one of the guys (I won't say his name, but I'm pretty sure I know who did it, and you know who you are, you mutherfucker!) tickled the head of my penis which, evidently, caused it to go from semi to rigid erection. (And I didn't even wakeup!)

That incident, occurrence—*whatever*!—got me the nickname of "Horsecock." And *other* derivatives I won't mention.

And it stuck.

Which brings me back to the ship's party and the other time I felt violent toward a shipmate. Two, in fact. (And these guys are not named and are not mentioned anywhere else.)

Of course the nickname was all in fun and ninety-nine-point-ninety-nine percent of the time it was used in fun and I took it in fun. Except this one time. I don't particularly like one of my bosses. Not liking him didn't mean I couldn't/wouldn't work for him. On board. On liberty it was a different matter.

At a ship's party it was really a different matter.

Sometimes talk led to actions, and if booze was involved, well...actions can sometimes cause re-actions. Anyway, this boss I didn't particularly like, and his buddy, another boss I was approaching not liking, and of course using my "nickname,"—*derogatorily,* no less, at least in a manner I didn't appreciate—got one on each side of me, then each got on one of my ears. One blowing, the other sucking.

This is too much!

I grab each of them and attempt to slam their heads together. And

I think I do get at least a piece of each of them. This ends their antics.

This also ends my days aboard the USS Carbonero.

I request a transfer and I get it. But, with less than a year to go in my naval career I am required to extend my original kitty cruise for one year. Now, instead of getting out the day before my twenty-first birthday, it will be the day before my twenty-second.

The USS Archerfish AGSS311, is in port and they need a torpedoman. I hear they're an all-bachelor crew. Sounds interesting. I go for it.

But first, I need to go somewhere else, back to civilian life after the Navy.

13

TRAVELS & PHILOSOPHIES

After the unhappy first farm auction, which I haven't mentioned too much, I try trade school. I mean, after all, after putting four years in the military, I do have the G.I. Bill. But I don't know what I want to do, and waste three months studying electrical technology, then three more months in junior college. (Not that any education is a waste of time, but, I felt, if I didn't have a goal, why waste the money, even government money.) In Jr. College at the ND State School of Science (NDSSS) I study government, speech, geology, and get a big fat **D** in trigonometry. I'm pretty sure I didn't even earn the **D**, as I have barely a clue as to what happens in trigonometry.

To make a long boring story short I also bounced around to several jobs: Floral and greenhouse, movie projectionist (I showed PLANET OF THE APES with CHARLETON HESTON eighteen times, since have bought the movie and watched probably thirty more times); car battery recycler (the very first day I got acid on my coveralls; the next day they fell apart and I quit, probably the shortest job I've ever had.) No, wait, there was one shorter: I had just been hired by the sugar beet plant in Moorhead, Minnesota, through the employment office. I drove onto the parking lot, at least started to enter the main building, then got a real good whiff of...whatever it is that smells bad at sugar beet plants, turned around and didn't even report for work. After that I worked in a couple other factories, worked for farmers, laid sod, but nothing was as thrilling as my past Navy adventures. Who knew?

****

Arizona started looking good. So one day I pack up my 59 Ford and take off.

I make it almost to Mount Rushmore by the first night. An open gate leads into some farmer's pasture so I swing in to sleep, and visit the four granite faces early the next morning. Many, many nights I spend in my car, the only problem being finding a private and safe place to take the chance of closing my eyes.

Custer State Park, also South Dakota, is next. One minute I'm on a regular highway, go around a curve, and there is a prairie dog town, a mule deer, and a herd of buffalo. It was as if I had stepped back two hundred years.

Wyoming and Yellowstone National Park come next. I don't see even one bear. Then Colorado and Rocky Mountain National Park. There is a beaver dam and pond and then a narrow and scary road up the mountain, which soon got icy. (And this is June, probably about 1968.) I remember being petrified behind the wheel, looking off to my right (or my left, I don't remember) but looking at the far snow-capped mountain peaks across the valley. Oh, yeah, and I'm going slow and cars are piling up behind me. I don't know if they are just being patient with me, or if they appreciate going so slow, or if they are mad, but finally one guy in a red sports car just can't take it any longer and passes everybody. Later I see skid marks. No, I don't stop to see if he has gone over the side. Finally we reach a turnoff and you can bet I pull in.

Going down is just as bad, maybe worse, and cars pile up behind me again.

Then comes Albuquerque, New Mexico. There I finally stop at a motel. Mostly I park and sleep near the highway but out of sight. And I wasn't the only one; others would park right on highway shoulders.

Finally Arizona. I remember coming down from the mountains and suddenly being in the desert. I made that trip kind of quickly. After all, I wasn't just light-heartedly touring. I needed to make a living too.

Which is no easier in Arizona. My first job is construction. They're building a corral for feeder cattle. I get a very short course on running a metal-cutting torch, and then start doing it. I sleep on site. On weekends the car becomes a furnace, and I have to keep the windows rolled up because of the unbelievable number of flies.

Next comes Winslow, Arizona. No job. Then Tucson, where I work as janitor at an all-night drive-in restaurant. I had just finished sweeping. I remember the assistant manager cutting onion rings into what looked to me like a garbage can. It wasn't. I can still see the look on his face after I dump my dust pan.

Then comes Phoenix. I join a bunch of magazine sales-people. You know the kind: They post this great classified ad: Great job: Great pay: Meet new people: Travel: Be your own boss. Then it's a twelve-hour day, you finally return to the motel, eat, and, oh, yeah, you're locked in with your "team". You're not exactly *locked* in, but they make you sell your car (if you have one; mine I kept long enough to be sure I didn't want to work for these people), then they quickly change cities and hold back your first pay so that one loses easy communication with your local loved ones. Some of the stories I heard suggested many were embarrassed to contact loved ones, so, in a *vague* way they actually became slaves. Kids, please, don't fall for those great-sounding ads.

I don't last long at any of the jobs. I finally run out of money, have to sell my car anyway, loose most of my possessions, and end up hitch-hiking home. Oh, yeah, and once high up in the mountains I almost had a fit because I had to pay $.45/gallon for gas. Wow. What we wouldn't give for $.45/gallon gas today.

I don't want to hitch-hike across Phoenix so I take a bus to Las Cruces, New Mexico. Unfortunately, the depot is on the wrong end of town so I have to walk through town, but Las Cruces is small compared to Phoenix. It's about 2 A.M. A city cop sees me, stops, then gives me my first ride, but only to the other end of town.

Looking back at that occurrence kind of reminds me of the movie FIRST BLOOD, with SYLVESTER STALLONE, only my cop was a good guy.

Now I am alone. Really, alone. It's dark, the few cars rush past me without even slowing (I don't blame them); it's one of those periods in life one does not forget.

I walk ten miles before getting a ride. At one point I was on a raised roadbed with ditches far below; a semi passes so closely that for those few seconds I don't know if I'll be blown off the road or sucked into the semi. I know I walked ten miles that day because a sign post says such-and-such a town 30 miles, then much later another sign says such-and-such a town 20 miles. Then I get a string of good rides; one is through a really beautiful area of sand dunes. Another is with a bunch of young Native Americans. The last one is with two men about in their late twenties who have been vacationing in Mexico. They spend their nights sleeping by the highway too, but they take me clear to Kansas City, right up to the bus depot, because I have just enough money to buy bus fare home from there.

These were two nice guys, but the situation, their look, their manner, our geographical location at the end: KANSAS, all reminded me of another movie, I, as a projectionist, showed umpteen times: TRUMAN CAPOTE'S IN COLD BLOOD.

After I get home it's soon winter. And Winslow, Arizona, soon makes national news with about ten feet of snow. I guess I am lucky to be not still there.

Looking at these pages, at the life I've led, I have to wonder sometimes, has God been with me, keeping me alive and healthy and, basically, out of trouble, for all these years, for some unknown reason, that I have yet to discover what is?

****

Then comes the second farm auction, the really unhappy one. This time we sell the land and buildings too. I say to my dad the day of the sale: "We could have made it." He answers: "I wish you had said that yesterday."

We both meant what we said, but I think we both also knew we were on borrowed time. In the early seventies values were beginning to go nuts. We had a little of this to sell and a little of that. It likely would have been just a matter of time. Giving up the farm meant the beginning of a long slow slide into emotional darkness. It would take years for me to get to the very bottom, but I *do* get there. And that will be the second to last chapter.

****

But first another trip: Washington state.

What possesses me on that day to leave home and family, *again*, with only a hundred dollars and a MOBILE OIL credit card, I will never know. As has been my life story, I do not spend much time with decision-making; if the desire is within me then usually nothing prevents me from following my wishes. My escapade begins May 31, 1974, and ends sixty days later, July 30, 1974. I had under my belt, nine states, six jobs, 6000 miles, one set of tires, scores of adventures, and sixty pages of hand-written journal. (In those days we hadn't yet even *dreamt* of laptops.)

Day one takes me west across my home state of North Dakota. It's misty, but the sky clears before I reach the color-hued hills of the Badlands, Theodore Roosevelt National Park. From miniature pieces of limestone to giant hills, the land here has been eroded and then sculptured , only the hills aren't really hills. The tops of the hills and buttes were once the land, but eons have decayed them into colorful testaments of time.

Leaving the highway I turn onto a dusty side road. The first thing I see is a solitary bull buffalo only about ten feet away. I stop my car (a 67 red Pontiac Tempest, a *cherry* car! [No, I don't still have it]). This majestic beast pays me no more attention then a passing gnat. After a moment though he did grumble a warning: "*I'm king on this hill, and nothing else.*" I don't argue, and move on.

The covey of grouse I see later are not so apathetic at my passing. They burst from the road like a scattering of buckshot, including their speed, and land in a short flight to blend perfectly with the ground. Honest to God, they are only a short distance away but I cannot see them.

A prairie dog town is next. I stop and watch…and philosophize. Sorry, but on this trip I did do some philosophizing. I promise to make the philosophizing short and not hold you up too often.

The meek will not inherit the earth. Left alone they will only destroy the Earth, and themselves. They will overpopulate until there is no room, overeat until no food, overeverything until nothing. The meek have no rules. They need the strong not to make rules but to enforce the already-present, natural rules.

Man will not inherit the earth for he is the meekest of all. Man tries to be perfect, but when something becomes perfect there is no longer any need for its continued presence, so will cease to be. Man must learn from the prairie dog. The prairie dog will overeat and overpopulate until it must move on to survive, but there is no place to move to, and to remain is to perish. Man with his intelligence and prairie dog with its instinct are both going by the same way.

****

Moving on….

The Burning Coal Vein sounds interesting so I follow the twisting dusty road for the extra six miles. Along the final route, which must be walked, I spy the color blue.

Sorry, more philosophizing:

Yellow, violet, green, brown, even red, common colors of the Badlands, but Blue! Blue stands out and hits one in the face when it appears and one must climb through the fence and struggle up the hill to get closer. I wonder, what did the first reasoning creature think and feel when he/she first saw Blue?

I had envisioned a flaming inferno inside maybe a cavern, like an eternal furnace. What greeted me was a wisp of smoke curling out of what appeared to be solid ground, and there is, basically, no hint of a flame. But smoke proves a fire is present. And the area is fenced, likely because of the danger of a possible cave-in.

On leaving I meet another lone male traveler. We nod and speak, which is usual for people meeting in out-of-the-way

places. He gets back to the entrance nearly as quickly as me and as we both enter our cars he states: "I think they're crazy!" Obviously he meant, in a very few words: ***"Why do they think that's great, that we should make a twelve-mile round trip, just to see some smoke?"*** **No doubt he missed the significance of the area, the fact that lightening struck the ground many years ago and ignited the coal beneath the ground, and that we humans are allowed the privilege of witnessing the forces of nature vividly at work.**

Why cannot man open his eyes and acknowledge the beauty everywhere, from the minute crystal of silica in sand to an immense mountain, from the tiniest flower on a grass stem to a full-blown rose, from the hundreds of forms of flora and fauna in a vacant city lot to a wide-spreading wildlife refuge; but, no, we hurry by, we do not take the time to partake of the natural tranquilizer for the mind and energizer for the body and soul. The excuse "*Someday I will.*" is getting old.

We cannot afford to wait until someday, because Mother Earth *will* not.

At Yellowstone, I, again, see no bears. (Just once I have seen a bear in the wild. Itasca State Park in Minnesota. I was riding a ferry on Itasca Lake and there appeared a bear on the near shore, and that boy/girl could move; I was thankful not to have met him/her on a hiking trail.)

At Old Faithful geyser, people are just gathering to witness the hourly spectacle. We wait. Kids and adults both are getting restless. Is it possible that the forces of nature have chosen this moment to work changes in the earth, to maybe release the pressure downward, instead of upward, or, worse yet, to go only a few feet into the air? But, no. Soon water and steam begins to gurgle and spit and Mother Nature releases her frustrations far into the air. The crowd is pleased, and leaves.

On leaving I notice a small herd of elk mostly oblivious to the eruption spectacle and completely ignoring the signs that tell us humans to stay on the boardwalks. They are grazing and resting as near to the geysers and fumaroles as they please. They also have left deposits on the boardwalks and roadways to remind us humans that this land is their land, and we humans are mere visitors.

The elements oxygen and hydrogen combine to form the compound, water. Around every bend water is found in some form at Yellowstone. It hisses as a fumarole, flows as a gentle creek, madly as a river, stupendously from a waterfall, or waits serenely silent as a pond.

I search for a campsite. Gibbon Falls. I stop.

The scene is chilling, almost frightening as dim light exhibits the white cascading water. I imagine a giant hand holding onto the rocks, as though trying to climb out of limbo.

Mammoth Hot Springs:

What giant played here and gouged the earth to bring forth the mineral-colored water that through eons has built these huge mounds that have spread over the land destroying all life and then stopping and allowing life to return?

The Morning Glory pool gives the impression of no bottom. The water is clear and allows me to see into its glassy darkness.

I remember pools of water during boyhood days that people claimed were bottomless. One dried up one summer and exposed its bottom, disproving the claim. The other never raised or lowered except during spring thaw or much rain. Most likely it was bottom-fed by a spring. However, the theory of no bottom was never decided. According to legend, two old men rowed out to the middle and lowered a weight, but they ran out of string. The number of feet on that ball of string somehow got lost in the transition of speech, so no one knows for sure, and no scientists have come to investigate.

My theory is, fine, let it be bottomless.

****

My last stop at Yellowstone is Tower Falls. I am pleased to be the only one here. I find a trail leading down, and, as I pick my way, the scene gradually changes.

Here, high in the Yellowstone, there is the air of a tropical rain forest. Ferns, lichens, mosses, are everywhere among the trees. The air is damp and hangs heavily with the stench of rotting vegetation. But it is a good smell: Mother Nature is returning her protégé to the earth, where they will nourish the plants of another generation, and, in turn, they too, will return whence they came.

I lose sight of the trail at times. It must not be used too often. I can't see the falls but its roar is constantly getting louder…and, then, the watery fireworks:

A pot of gold appears at my feet, the end of a rainbow, a full rainbow, appearing and disappearing depending on the mood of the falling water and the whims of the breeze and the attitude of the sun. The roar is tremendous, the spray is cold, the sun is bright. I stand in awe, caught up by the excitement and the fury, dwarfed by the sights and sounds. There would be no survival in that boiling, churning water.

I spend twenty-four hours touring Yellowstone. A month would be better. I believe Yellowstone is like a woman. One must fully understand her in order to know her and be able to fully appreciate her. Another time I compare nature to a woman. I have always wondered, why do I love being in a canoe so much. Finally one day it comes to me. I have just stepped into an aluminum canoe, and have felt it give. No, the bottom of the canoe doesn't give; it's the sensation of the water giving beneath the canoe. It's what one feels becoming attached with the water-filled body of a woman, it's the giving of her breasts, her stomach, and her thighs, all, giving.

Something I have learned about Yellowstone, now, thirty-five years later, is somewhat unsettling. She sits above maybe the biggest —but, for now, *quiet*— volcano in the world. I don't want to even *think* about what could happen if she ever decides to go.

****

The miles through Idaho fly past quickly. Evidently I am in a hurry to get…I don't know where, just somewhere else. My car overheats.

At Twin Falls, Idaho, I stop for repairs. Upon leaving I see a hitchhiker at the freeway entrance. Possibly I give some indication I am going to stop, for he reaches for his bag just as I'm making the turn onto the ramp. I realized later that he had made a well-planned move, likely well-rehearsed too, because it worked, for I stopped.

For the next several miles there is much talk. I tell him my problems and he tells me his. With very little influence I change my plans (that I didn't have anyway) and decide to take him to Portland, Oregon. In return he will give me names and locations where I can find work in the fruit harvest. Fourteen hours later, at 2 A.M., we arrive.

When morning comes we locate his father who is homesteading just outside the city among nurseries and orchards. I'm somewhat shocked at his father's appearance, as the man's skin appears to be moldy, but, on somewhat closer inspection, I realize his skin is covered with tattoos that have lost their colors and now are just blue lines. The man's eyes give me the impression that I am being looked into and not at: He knows who I am, what I am, and whether or not I did it, and, I suspect, he's pretty sure I'm guilty as hell. We spend Sunday with him, in quiet solitude.

Our first job is a blood bank, actually a plasma bank. We get $5 each for a donation of one pint of blood: They remove the plasma, you get your red blood cells back, and God help you if you get someone else's.

That afternoon we visit one of his old friends, a giant of a black man, who, is now, and has been for twenty years, chained to a wheelchair with crippling arthritis. Even so he washes himself, cooks for himself, and cares for his chickens and guinea hens. When we leave there are no goodbyes. It is good to come and say "Hi" but it is easier to go by not saying "Goodbye."

That night we cross the Columbia River to Vancouver, Washington. I'm told (as if I am the rider and he is the driver) that we are headed for Pasco, where he is sure they are by now pulling rye out of certified wheat fields. We arrive too late for work so we enter a mission for the night. For a free bed, shower, and meal, there is the small price of listening to a sermon.

After the free shower and meal (the bread was moldy) I retire to my car for the night. The next morning I'm awake early, as usual. Three men arrive, one pushing a bicycle. I walk toward them and are greeted: "Hey, buddy, did you wake up with a cigarette this morning?" I pass out my cigarettes (they were cheaper then.)

Soon a farmer arrives looking for rye-pullers, at $2/hour. I go to the mission and get my rider and we all pour into the farmer's van. I hate leaving my car there alone. After all, it is my only real and true and dependable friend.

Endless miles and miles of wheat fields appear. We spread out approximately 75 feet apart and start through the field. Mostly we walk. When rye appears, standing well above the wheat, we practically have to fight to see who will pull it. Come on, guys, this isn't piecemeal. Then we top a hill and there is enough rye to keep us all busy for an hour.

My rider gets one day of pay and doesn't show up the second day. The third day the farmer doesn't show up either. I find my rider in a bar. I tell him I'm leaving. He says OK. I don't remember this guy's name. I do kind of remember his face and general appearance. I still have the blanket he left in my car. I have heard different men discussing Wenatchee, where they are probably thinning apple trees by now.

I move on, alone.

****

At the Wenatchee employment office I am immediately sent out. Turns out the farmer wanted only "experience", but, he would let me "try out." The 70-year-old trees tower into the sky. I am sure he won't want the top branches thinned, but he does. I am leery of standing at the top of a sixteen-foot folding ladder but I decide to give it a try. After two hours he comes back to see how I am doing. "Not good," but then "Not bad, either," and "way too slow." But he decides to let me stay the day "For coming." At the end of the day he hands me a check and seems almost apologetic, sorry that he couldn't hire me.

"Tell you what," he says, "Go back to the employment office

and ask for someone with dwarf trees, and, maybe, about the third place, they'll let you stay on." He extends his hand, "Good luck!" A good man.

I check the paper. There are many thinning jobs available. I call one and get directions. He doesn't sound too friendly, "Be there at 7 A.M. and we'll try you out." With no place to spend the night I decide to follow the directions to the apple orchard. There is a bunkhouse. A worse-looking hole to live in I have never seen, and there are people living there. I do decide to partake of a shower. I take just one look and wonder, *do I really want to stand on those wooden slats, and without shower shoes?* (I should have listened to myself, for I develop the worst case of athlete's foot that I ever hope to have.) I decide to stay with my car.

I meet a lot of people on my trip to Washington. I meet a true hippie (Hey, it's the seventies!); we spent a lot of time philosophizing, but him I'm not going to tell you about. There simply was too much. Rather I'll tell you about "Sid" a "rubber" tramp. That means he is a tramp with "wheels." (Sort of like me.) Sid and his buddy had a five-passenger camper pickup with the works: Two televisions, elaborate stereo system, refrigerator, stove, double bed…they had it made, set for life. Then, like the snapping of a finger but in slow-motion—disaster! The semi ahead was jack-knifing, no place to go but into him and another semi from behind compresses them like an accordion. Sid, who was driving, was mainly unhurt. His buddy, who was sleeping in back, received a piece of glass in the mouth which tore a four-inch gash and knocked out most of his teeth, hips were crushed, jaw broken, collarbone broken, three fingers lost. His buddy is finished as a tramp.

As for Sid, "What the heck? I started with nothing…."

****

Badger Mountain Lookout (Fire Tower). On the way there I notice the sky and stop:

The sun behind the clouds is no more than a dull yellow disc, the clouds are smooth and snowy white with somewhat jagged edges, but also somewhat rounded on the edges like a

gigantic, *animated*, bolt of lightening with no end and across the whole top of the sky. In the immediate vicinity of the sun there are many colors: Yellow, blue-green, dark pink, and many others; they are in a swirl like an oil slick on water. As I watch, the colors spread over the edges of the clouds into blue sky until they cover twenty times the original area. Soon the cloud cover leaves the sun. The colors begin to disappear until there is nothing and the sun is again bright.

During the display I removed my sunglasses for a few seconds and the colors were barely discernible. I'm sure my naked eye would have missed the display entirely. I considered what I saw as a daytime aurora borealis. Years later I find a photograph: The phenomenon is called **IRIDESCENCE**.

Following signs I move on toward the lookout tower. The road gradually worsens until there is just one track. Ahead the road leads around a knob and appears to end right there. I have a vision of the road caving in and dumping me back the thousands of feet I have just climbed, or the road ending with a sheer drop-off, or meeting someone and one of us having to back up. (It wouldn't have been me!) None of these things happen and soon the tower comes into view.

I climb the tower. A slight, stooped, white-haired old man is in charge. He gives me a panoramic tour, points out familiar landmarks 20-30 miles away, and informs me he has already reported a lightening-started fire that day. I thank him and climb back down, and decide to explore the nearby rock piles.

As my eyes make out the yellow and black jagged rings every muscle in my body tenses as I freeze in stark terror. I am observing my first rattlesnake in the wild. Enough wind has prevented me from hearing its warning buzz. (I'm assuming it *did* give me a warning.) Only because I am studying the ground did I see it. My body relaxes slightly and I move forward. The scaly body of the snake moves further back into the rocks, and stops when I do. (Oh, wait, it's probably just retracting so that it can strike!) I move slightly forward again. The snake moves again and exposes its rattler, definitely rattling, but the wind

again prevents me from hearing. I freeze again, and can now see the flicking movement of its forked tongue. The snake's head is facing me directly, but my mind tells me I want to get still closer, to not give in to fear and waste this moment. Forcing myself I move closer. The snake recoils still more...one more step...more recoil. I'm now within five feet. This snake apparently feels this rock pile belongs to him, and will not retreat.

So, I do.

***

Upon returning to the lowlands I pass a waterway, and stop. Honest, when I pass some once-in-a-lifetime-moment I *must* stop.

The foaming, wild, raging, free spirit of the Entiat River rushes past me on its journey to the now-drowned Columbia. Inches below my feet is sudden and sure death. But my boulder is solid; it has been perched here for eons; surely erosion will not pick this moment to topple it. The nonliving massiveness of the boulder would not even notice the force and icy shock of the water, but then, in a few seconds, neither would I....

Silver Falls, Wenatchee National Forest.

Falling, splashing, churning, boiling, foaming from top to bottom the water is silvery-white, and crashing from the high Cascade Mountains, and woe to any who tries to stop it—a drop hits my face! That drop will evaporate and somewhere join with a cloud, and drop to the earth into the soil, then into a stream, then a river, finally to the ocean where it will again condense and enter the air to join another cloud...and someday, in its infinite travels will this particular molecule of water drop onto this same mountain to again go cascading down Silver Falls and splash onto somebody's face? *My* face?

Pioneer Village, Cashmere, Washington:

Like a gracious lady about to rise to greet a visitor who has just come in the door, the life-like mannequin rests in the old rocking chair. The Bible is in the process of being closed, the pages suspended. Here, time itself has been suspended, time for us to slow down, take a moment to look back and view a time

that was not so much in a hurry. People then strived to live as well as the land would allow them. Today the land is living as well as *we* will allow *it*.

I have spent a few weeks at this orchard. It has financed my local travels in this very beautiful part of Washington, but the owner of this orchard has not been satisfied with my work from day one, nor, probably, has he been satisfied with anything from the day he was born. (I'm probably condemning him without fair trial and later I'll be sorry for leaving.) I'm especially sorry for leaving the kind and generous foreman, the likes of which is likely not found in this fruit business too often. I mean produce has to be taken care of now, and quickly! I certainly don't question that. But I was getting itchy feet anyway. I head for Royal City, where I hear they're hiring cherry pickers.

I find a cherry orchard but too late for that day. "Come back tomorrow at 5 A.M." So I decide to spend some time at the nearby O'Sullivan Dam, where I find lots of litter and no litter barrel (trash was brought in, it could have been taken out!)

I do find some privacy, though, on a cluster of boulders right on the water's edge. Suddenly a seagull appears, swoops down and comes up with a fish. It is immediately pounced upon by a second seagull, whose action causes the fish to fall, only to be grabbed by a third bird. All the squawking appears to be a signal for a free-for-all, for, in the end, nine birds are involved, and the fish escapes.

The wind speed rises, changes direction, begins blowing water spray onto me. It's not bad though, so I keep sitting and enjoying the view. Shortly an old fisherman appears from around the bend, constantly casting and reeling in. Several minutes pass before he sees me. I wave, he nods. I would have liked to talk with him, but he soon turns and heads back the way he came. Did he feel as I did, that because this small cove was isolated, that the whole rocky shore would be? Was he, too, searching, hoping to find privacy from other human beings? I would say yes!

Cherry picking is not easy, as I soon find out. Ten hours later I have completed one tree. I am then informed that the old grandmother who started the same time as me has picked 13 boxes compared to my 4, or about $13 compared to my $4. The owner says I would probably catch on in five or six days, but in the meantime he will keep his ladders full of professionals. (Oh, yeah, right, I wonder how many cherries that old grandmother ate. Probably none. But I ate plenty.)

I decide to head for Spokane, the World's Fair, and to visit my good friend from the Navy, Everett Wenke. (Everett will appear again in the last two naval chapters.) On the way I pass a sign: PLEASANT VALLEY. Does such a town really exist? Or was the sign put there as a cruel joke? I considered checking it out but didn't. I didn't want to take the chance of spoiling my idea of what might be there.

I spend one day at the World's Fair (including a helicopter ride); it was somewhat of an ordeal, as people were rushing everywhere, trying to see everything.

Slow down! Stop! Look! Listen! Feel the sights and sounds around you, absorb them, appreciate and enjoy them today, for you might never pass this way again. Slow down, so that you may *see* the bell tower, *see* the waterfalls, *see* the people around you and try to understand what things mean in their relationship to you. Stop, and *look* at something if it attracts your attention. A passing glance is not enough; you will always wonder and be unadmittedly sorry if you don't. Look, at everything, not just the center of attraction that reaches out and grabs you, but look at the smaller, more obscure things as well; they have their meaning also. Listen, don't just catch a fleeting word, don't move on in the middle of a sentence or even leave at the end of a paragraph, but stay, until the whole message has been presented to you. Feel, with your very soul all that goes on around you, your mind will throw out that which is unimportant; you won't get so full that you *runneth over.* Slow down, society, life is too sweet to rush through without ever knowing its infinite, and *intimate*, beauty.

Arriving at my friend's house I have surprised myself that I have found it without getting lost even once. In the yard is a young red-haired woman, (Nancy) holding a baby, and an older woman,

Nancy's grandmother, and a small dog. I feel welcome the moment I pull up. Soon Everett (I call him Wink, and he, of course, calls me Nell) arrives, driving an orange Fiat convertible, a very small car compared to the six-foot-six-inch frame driving it. A warm greeting is made and words fly for the next several minutes as we relive old times and the last eight years.

It's strange how some relationships never change. He is the same person I knew eight years ago. I haven't always found this to be true. As Wink said: "By the time you're 21, you have probably developed your life-long personality. If one is basically honest at 21, you aren't likely to turn into a crook later."

Right.

(In April, 2008, thirty-five years after that visit, Wink and Nancy visit me in my North Dakota home, and he is *still* the same guy I met in the Navy. Something has now changed, though. He's taking a trip around the country, by car and by plane, visiting family and old friends [I feel really honored to be included] but I fear this is to be a 'goodbye' trip, as he has developed prostate cancer. We continue to communicate by email.) (At 10pm, August 23, 2009, I receive an email from Nancy that my dear friend,Wink, has passed away.)

****

In the next several days, besides good conversation, we enjoy barbecues, a sports car rally, and a trip to Noisy Creek Campground on Sullivan Lake (*not* O'Sullivan Dam) in Colville National Forest for the 4th of July.

In preparation for the camping trip I restore and clean my car. In the process I remove the backseat and reorganize it. Now I'll be able to sleep comfortably with my feet in the trunk. Beats the hell out of curling up in the front seat.

That same day the grandmother has to return to Seattle. There is a touching scene between her and the baby:

Is there a love anywhere in the world compared to that which radiates from a grandmother to a baby grandchild? Life

can end for a grandmother at any time, simply due sometimes to old age, so she must give and hope to receive as much love as possible. A man can love his woman, a mother can love her baby, a father can love his son, a person can love their pet or their land or their country...endless possibilities...but, in all of these there is not the factor of time. Everything has a time allotment but usually it can be spread over a large area and many years. Only to a grandmother is love so precious and time so short.

Later, I too, am afflicted with this thing called "Baby love." Nancy has asked me to sit with her baby for about ten minutes while she takes her grandmother to the airport. The plane's schedule does not correspond with Wink's arrival from work:

The baby cries and I take her into my arms to comfort her. The gratifying emotion of love overwhelms me as I hold her small body against me. Her tiny hand grips my neck; her crying voice fills my ear. At this precise moment I am the *only* person able to see to her needs, a grave responsibility taken lightly by many.

That night it is decided the dog should have a bath before we go camping. Just the sound of the running water has sent the dog under the couch. What about every other time water is ran? How can he know, lying there with his ears flat, his big eyes looking sad, that *this* bath is for him? After the bath the dog runs about the house barking excitedly, evidently anticipating something. Wink throws a red ball. The dog retrieves it and enjoys the game immensely. So why is the bath such a punishment to the dog when it knows what comes immediately afterward?

I leave for the campground early to be sure we get a site. Early the next morning I sit by the glasslike lake, philosophizing, *again*:

Like a polished mirror the lake lay still, silent, untarnished except for the occasional ripple made by a surfacing fish. Almost imperceptibly a gentle movement begins on the other side of the lake and moves toward me, giving the impression of a glittery, silver-laden blanket being drawn over it. Completed, the water is again silent...or is it just giving the

notion of silence, for the edges continue to glitter, further spaced now, and longer, a thousand transparent lines with tiny voltages. Slowly the glittery lines become shorter, as the resistance of the water becomes stronger, forcing the voltage back into the shore. Does this glittering voltage make a daily journey across the lake charging the water with life, or do the lines gather energy from the water to regenerate life on land?

Later that day I am entranced by a rectangular growth of trees and bushes leading off to…?

An aisle into the forest is lined with snow-white young birch and older slate-colored balsam and interwoven with ferns. Burned-out stumps and rotting logs indicate what has been and what might lie ahead. On either side of the aisle the forest is open and admitting sunlight, but the aisle itself is dark, dank, repulsive, but its very repulsiveness has made it attractive, so enticing that a person could be drawn into its realms of fantasy. What would he find? Would it be an entrance to another world, a never-never land, or just an exit from this?

If one could see what lay ahead, and *liked* what he saw but could only go one way or the other, go in or stay out, would he go ahead and leave his present life behind?

Sorry, I didn't enter and find out. I was afraid it would be a fantasyland and I wouldn't want to return.

****

An interesting spot on the map is 6483-foot Sullivan Mountain, and the location of an operating fire lookout tower. According to the map there is a road leading all the way up…but we soon find the road getting worse and worse. We creep across one hazard only to find a worse one ahead. We come to a slanted rock slide covering the road. There are tracks crossing it but it's easy to imagine the whole mountain falling down. After a few minutes of consideration we decide not to continue, so now we must *back* down that road until we reach a place where we can turn around. (Thank God there *is* one.) *That* went well enough. We arrive back at the very worst spot. It is an outside curve and the road is wet from a spring running across it and it has caved away on the main point of the turn. Didn't we notice that on the way up?

Coming up the road I was on the inside (I couldn't see how close we were to the edge), but now I can. As we go into the tightest part of the turn I'm sure my heart stops as I watch the "road" disappear. For the first time in my life I believe I actually go into shock. I thought I could feel the rear of the car settling into the mud, and…but…at last: Solid ground. I take a breath and feel a new reverence for life.

We spend several days at this campsite, and I leave from the campsite. Parting is a sad affair for me, because Wink and I are as close as eight years earlier. I've come to believe that "Hello" is much better than "Goodbye." But my feet are getting itchy again: I *must* see what lies over the next hill.

****

How many days pass before I reach the Pacific Ocean I don't remember. I'm possibly getting tired of this constant run on the highways. I might even be getting homesick. I'm sure visiting Wink and his family helped cause this feeling to begin. I might even be running out of writing energy, as I'm cutting lots of scenes.

I reach Mount Rainer National Park, and guess what? I'm broke. I can't even afford the $2 entry fee. Luckily, when still several miles away I could see Mount Rainier and Mount Adams rising above the clouds. I'm not sure how I feel right now, kind of down. I need a job and I don't really want to get another one.

So, I move on.

The Palisades, Gifford Pinchot National Forest:

A gigantic library of ancient books: Enclosed within them are the untold stories of the centuries, the ages, the eons. In one form or another, these rocks were here when nothing else was, and will still be here when nothing else is.

Further down the road: Clear Creek Falls:

An eternal spray of white, foaming, blossoming, fireworks, cascades down the smooth rock drop. Actually a narrow creek it

widens at the head of the falls to let the rock wall show through. The water is feathery and sends an infinite number of droplets that blossom into upside-down parachutes that crash into several more falls before they finally reach the bottom and enter Clear Lake.

Nearing Natchez, Washington, I begin seeing many orchards and they still hang heavy with cherries. It has just rained so I'm told I maybe could go to work the next morning, so, as usual, I have some free time. I like being out in the country and "out of sight" (so to speak) when I stop to work. All police impress me with what they stand for and what they do, but I suffer from paranoia whenever they are around. I'm not breaking any law, but then I'm not exactly a first class hard-working citizen either. For instance, at this very moment I could easily be classed a vagrant.

Later I try to visit a "county" park:

There is a sign by a little building that reads "Stop" so I stop. A large girl saunters out and asks, "Are you here for all day?"

"No, I just want to visit for the afternoon."

"All right. 75 cents, please."

Since I have no experience with county parks this admission charge surprises me. Being broke, naturally I can't enter. I consider asking how much one hour would be. *(I've got 31 cents, damn it, and I want to spend it!)* Instead I simply admit to being broke. She answers with a shrug and saunters back into the little building.

I spend the rest of the day and night in the yard of the orchard where I'm going to "hopefully" work. (Some of you reading this must wonder how I survived. Fairly easy. I had a gas credit card, and, when I did have money, I stocked a large cooler with ice and groceries, plus I had a COLEMAN camp stove.)

Picking cherries is easy (earlier I said it wasn't, but it is) I mean, you pluck the little cherry from the stem and drop it into the bucket—what could be easier? The important thing, as I discovered before, is to develop speed. Oh, and don't eat all the profits! At the end of the day I thought I had done really well with 21 buckets. But the professionals had 40-60 buckets. Change that to dollars and you have a pretty good day's pay. (The buckets I estimate to hold three gallons.)

A couple more days and I again have some change, and the urge to move becomes strong again. The next day we don't pick and he has only a couple days left of harvest anyway, so, I collect my pay and leave.

Just when and how I decided, I don't know, but when I pulled out of that yard I knew I was heading in the general direction of home. I am still sorry for not seeing Mount Rainier up close, but, for some reason as I'm pulling onto the highway, I turn and glance over my right shoulder and, again, there she is: Mount Rainier in all her splendor rising above the clouds.

A picture, a flash, a memory, a knowledge strikes me that I've been here before, and I have been, but not in the flesh. Back in Wenatchee I had lain half awake but asleep enough to dream: There is a sharp curve around the mountainside. I'm on the inside lane against solid rock. The outside lane has a guard rail and then a sheer drop. A semi comes around the curve and starts to buckle, taking the whole road—no place for me to go…shaking and afraid I wake from the dream. Now, about one month later, I am here, at the actual location of my dream. As I round the curve my hands tighten on the wheel. But there is no semi. You remember Sid, right, the "rubber" tramp? I probably had this dream not too long after talking to him.

Later that day, on the same highway, I come close to realizing that dream, but under slightly different circumstances:

The road curves sharply to my left. Long before I know for sure my hands tighten on the wheel and my foot eases toward the brake. My senses have somehow told me that the oncoming car is in my lane. As he goes into the curve I see dust and gravel flying, *confirming*—he's not in my lane but on the *shoulder* of my lane. My left foot, already on the brake—that's how I learned: Left foot for the brake—began putting on slight pressure in an attempt to avoid what might be coming. It's a short stretch of old highway where the freeway hasn't yet been completed, and this driver, probably in a very relaxed condition, has likely forgotten that he, and not the freeway, is in control of the car. Also, the sun

is in his eyes and he's going too fast: Just a bad set of conditions present. He regains some control and gets his car back onto the highway but now he's coming directly toward me. We both have a decision to make. His is simple: Turn into your lane, *now*! Mine is not so simple: I can take the ditch, go into his lane, or keep going straight and see if I can hit him harder than he hits me! In this instant in time one cannot make a decision and then try to change it. There is no time. I put more pressure on my brakes and steer slightly toward the ditch. It's gesture enough. The other driver yanks his wheel and gets into his own lane. The collision is avoided. Neither of us stop. What could be said? Our destinies have been fulfilled: We both turned our wheel in the correct direction.

Going home I revisit some of the same places I saw on the Arizona trip, including Wind Cave National Park in South Dakota. I was hoping for some of the same thrill as before, but, alas, I can't seem to experience the same thrill twice. I used to, back on the farm. I could go to the exact same spot every day, even more than once in a day, and feel good about it every time. I could also go to the same spots in the nearby woods, or country lanes, even to my church in the wildwood, and I would look forward to it.

But at Wind Cave it didn't happen. The first time I came around a bend it was like passing a gate and returning to the 1800s. The same for Mount Rushmore. The first time I arrived at the memorial in full dark so I was at the viewpoint at first light, and alone. As daylight arrived the likenesses of the presidents' faces were gradually brought out. I was truly enthralled. This time I arrived at 9 A.M. and there was a stone-faced ranger directing traffic. As was necessary. I didn't stay long.

From Mount Rushmore I resume my flight home. I stop at WALL DRUG but there are so many people I don't even try to enter. Returning to the freeway I see two hitchhikers. I pick them up. Two young men, I would guess in their early twenties. They are from Colorado en route to Missouri for a rock festival. They each have a bedroll, a small canteen of water between them, and no money. For awhile I wonder, what possessed these two boys to take off like this, but I soon realize that the only difference between them, and me, is that I have a car and a credit card.

****

And that was how it went, especially on the Washington trip: Escape: Escape your home: Escape your job: Escape your life: Escape from people! Privacy, even forty years ago was fast becoming a dirty word. We think we have to grow: Grow the population: Grow the economy: Get bigger and bigger: Charge more taxes to serve and support the growing population to pay those taxes, and then grow some more and charge even more taxes. It's a mad cycle that cannot go on forever.

On a very personal note it's discouraging and frustrating to me to see Fargo leapfrogging south, in my general direction, and bringing their rules, suburban lawns, mosquito spray, free-ranging dogs, demands for city-like services, the list goes on.

Fargo's latest leap on I-29 adds three more miles south of Exit 60 to a sign announcing "Future Home of Rutten Park". I mean, how much growth do these people want? I remember a small billboard (back in the fifties, or so) on the south edge of Fargo at the intersection of University Drive and 13th Avenue South (then a gravel road); the sign said "40,000 friendly people welcome you."

I'm probably far enough away; they will never swallow me, but what about other people that live on the outskirts? What about farms that have been there since the beginning? I'm sure there are some others who also feel horrified seeing Fargo yet in the distance but getting closer and closer. And, by the way, paving over some of the richest land—not just in the nation—but the world. What do the powers that be want, anyway? A MEGALOPOLIS from Grand Forks to Wahpeton? Maybe so.

But I shouldn't make it sound like Fargo is alone. Every little town, in the nation, probably, is desperate to grow. The theory seems to be Grow or become Extinct.

Sorry to be getting negative, folks, but whenever and wherever I have ever gone to look for solitude, instead I have found tail-gators, litterers, boom boxes, dirt bikes, barking dogs, etc., etc., so, I'm going to end this chapter and return to 1965 and my rewarding naval career. Thanks for listening.

There was one other trip I should mention that stands out. It was about in 1956 or 57; I was eleven or twelve, and I went with my late-great Grandpa Johnson (my mother's father) on a GREYHOUND BUS to Stevens Point, Wisconsin, to visit my Uncle Earl, Aunt Inez and my cousins Kenny and Tommy. We took several bicycle rides (once to Mosquito Bluff) hauled bales, visited Whispering Pines, and listened to whippoorwills at night. And rocks. That country had the prettiest rocks, and I collected them along Buena Vista Creek, and brought them all home (I still have them.) But we didn't have a lot of room in our luggage. Not to worry. I got them all in. I even filled my grandpa's extra shoes with rocks. And, yes, the bus driver commented on the weight of our luggage. I wonder today if we could even get away with such a thing.

Much as I enjoyed that trip, I would almost hate to go back today, because all those beautiful places will be changed. You know what I mean, they'll be improved, updated, more civilized, sometimes just "cleaned" up.

Ken is the only one still with us. My good friend and cousin Tommy went to Vietnam. He didn't get killed in Vietnam but he came home all changed, so, maybe in that respect, we did lose him there.

14

USS ARCHERFISH

There's a reason for the all-bachelor crew, and when somebody gets married they automatically get transferred. The USS Archerfish AGSS311 is an oceanographic survey ship, complete with civilian scientists. Their home port is Pearl Harbor, same as Carbonero's, but they are almost never home. They go everywhere, and where they are going next is Bremerton, Washington, for a six-month yard period. One of the big jobs at the shipyard will be removal of their ten no longer used torpedo tubes. Their only armament now will be six Thompson submachine guns, three M-1 rifles, and ten semiautomatic .45 caliber pistols.

The Thompson submachine gun, now there is a nice weapon. The first time I fired it, I must have been screwing up royally (not again!) so the instructor, without my knowledge, flipped it onto full automatic, then told me to pull the trigger and he put his hand against my back and held me steady as my finger basically froze to the trigger as I emptied the clip. I remember the gun crawling skyward but I did keep it mostly down and mostly under control, thanks to his hand on my back.

As torpedoman my billet will be care of those small arms, and in charge of what is no longer the After Torpedo Room but now the

After Room, strictly for sleeping.

Every city has its own Submarine bar. At Bremerton it's the Crow's Nest. But I'm still underage in most states. I make it into the Crow's Nest just once. So, most of my liberties consist of ferryboat rides across Puget Sound to Seattle, library visits and zoo visits. About the most exciting thing that happens is a small earthquake while Archerfish is in dry dock. That could have become *very* exciting had the gate that keeps the water out shook loose, and especially since I was on the gangplank at the time, half in, half out.

At least I got to experience an earthquake.

I did run into an old friend from home in Bremerton, Charles Stenseth. We also bumped into each other in the chow line at boot camp, where we yelled "Hi!" to each other and that was about it. No time for visiting. Our job at the mess hall was to eat and get back to the barracks. I found out later that Charles had enlisted a couple weeks after me. Even though we couldn't visit it was still good to see a familiar face.

After the yard period the shakedown cruise takes us to San Francisco. Again, at least the first night, most everybody goes to the sub bar. (Don't remember the name.) Right, I'm still underage but occasionally I chance it. This night I get through the door, where I casually mention I have not yet drank my dolphins.

Mistake. Brothers, Jack and Frank Ely are some of those who hear, and likely Terry Allen, and Johnny Foley, and Archie Moore. No, not the boxer, but I'm sure he could have held his own in most any fight. There was another special adventure with Archie. We were in Yokosuka (yes, the Archerfish went there too.) Archie and I had made our rounds of the streets the night before and paid for it with hangovers the next morning, and that's when the adventure occurred. For some reason, unknown to any but God, Archie slipped and fell overboard. Well, he got out OK, but when he got to me, he evidently figured that I had pushed him overboard, so, he pushed me. I hit the water and went under. Now, remember, I have never claimed to be a good swimmer, and, right now, I have a hangover. As I struggle to the surface for the third time I have this mind-picture-memory of Terry Allen jumping in to save me. Thank you, Terry

Allen. I will never, ever, forget you.

The message about not yet drinking my dolphins flashes around the bar at about forty knots. Soon a glass is found about the size of a large milkshake. Too bad it won't be a milkshake in it. First my dolphins are removed and dropped into the bottom of the glass. It's a long way down. Then alcohol of every description is poured into the glass. Probably a little beer too, you know, a beer for the chaser. Finally a few small chunks of ice.

Then the glass is slid to me.

"You have to drink it without stopping, Nelly, and then catch your dolphins in your teeth." (I don't remember who said this.) "If you stop, you not only have to finish that drink but you have to drink another, and another...until you finish without stopping."

Well, they don't know what a great drinker they're talking too. I pick up the glass, study for a moment my dolphins nestled safely at the bottom, put the glass to my lips and begin drinking. And drinking. And I hear cheers and rooting, "Go, Nelly! Go, Nelly!" And I keep drinking, and drinking. Finally, ice chunks are falling from the glass past my cheeks as I keep the liquid going into my mouth, and at last, my dolphins, in my teeth!

A great cheer, "Yea, Nelly!"

One good drink always calls for another. I order a beer and sit at the bar with my good friend Everett Wenke. We discuss something or other. I spot a bright red dress nearby and shiny black hair. I ask her to dance. I hold her close. I have this last memory of holding this lovely senorita in a slow dance…just before I hit the floor.

Only about two or three minutes have passed since drinking my dolphins.

The next morning I am lying flat on my face and puking straight in the air, with no memory of anything in between.

Great drinker. Right.

****

Sometime during the cruise back to Pearl Harbor we hold drills. I'm sitting in the After Room with the sound-powered phones headset on. An officer comes back. I won't mention his name because I am about to ruin his day. I knew there were drills being conducted but so far they had not pertained, directly, to me. Maybe I had forgotten. Maybe I was bored. I have no excuse for what happens next, so, forty years later I will take full blame. But responsibility? No, I'm sorry, I can't take responsibility. The responsibility always lies with the senior officer present.

He tells me, "Nelson, there is a pencil-sized leak—"

And that's all the further I let him get.

"Flooding in the After Room!" I announce over the headset, "Flooding in the After Room!"

I can only imagine what happens up in the Conning Tower and Control Room, but about two seconds later the word comes over the intercom, "Flooding in the After Room! Flooding in the After Room! Surface! Surface! Surface!"

RrrrUuuugha! RrrrUuuugha! RrrrUuuugha!

And up we go.

I don't know how many of you have seen the emergency surface by the USS Dallas in that great movie THE HUNT FOR RED OCTOBER, with SEAN CONNERY, but that fine nuclear submarine came from the depths with about a 45 degree up angle. Well, so did we, but we didn't have the use of Hollywood props. In the movie nothing (or not much) tipped over or spilled. Not so on the USS Archerfish.

The men in Conn and Control didn't know that a blockhead had jumped the gun. They didn't know that there was no flooding at all. All they knew was that the word came over the phones, "Flooding in the After Room!"

So they had to react accordingly and bring that sub to the surface as quickly as possible. The up angle was so steep that everybody had to hang on. Pots and pans, bedrolls and card games went rolling and flying. And oil drip pans emptied their loads. One emptied on that poor officer and he had no choice but to stand there hanging on and letting it happen. He probably still has post traumatic stress syndrome over that incident. Of course, I was hanging on for dear life too, but no drip pan was pouring oil on me. I don't remember for sure if I actually laughed, but I know I was choking off a grin.

Because, yes, it was funny in its own way.

But what a dumbass I was.

I didn't apologize to that officer then, so I'd like to do so now. I'm very, very, sorry for that incident, Sir. I was really, *really*, a dumbass.

Whether there were recriminations for the officer from that incident I don't know. Not one person ever talked to me about it. Maybe the officers, the other officers, the ones who didn't get oil dumped on them, appreciated such a realistic drill.

15

TEST OF WILL POWER

One more detour before we get to the end. One more major thing that has happened to me. August 1980, I volunteered to live just under six months at the Human Nutrition Research Center (HNRC) at Grand Forks, North Dakota. This is close to thirty years ago. Things there have changed, I'm sure, probably a lot, but I will tell this story how it happened to me, how it was when I was there.

Eleven A.M. Monday morning. A nicotine craving stabs the back of my head. Seconds later it thrusts into my chest, along with a growing desire for COKE, chocolate, syrup-drenched pancakes—*something*! And that wild-eyed craving is how I feel every day, sometimes several times a day, and sometimes seemingly-continually throughout the whole day. And nicotine is not the only thing. Once craving begins there follows a full circuit of COKE, coffee, chocolate, maple syrup, chewing gum, bacon and eggs, and butter-saturated toast, even my favorite toothpaste—I've even begun craving licking my own postage stamps, but no, staff has to do it for me.

But I have agreed to abstain from mortal pleasures. I stare at my bed, shelves, a scatter rug, a bright window facing north framing the green crown of an eighty-foot cottonwood. Many times I would stare at that giant tree, thinking of solitude. Once a crow attacked a resting great horned own in the tallest branches.

Outside my door is prescribed diet, shower and exercise facilities, a pool table, television, stereo, nurses, a psychologist, medical doctors, microbiologists, nutritionists…just about anything the other research volunteers and I could desire.

Except freedom.

No leaving the laboratory living quarters without a chaperone, no candy, favorite toiletries, tobacco, alcohol, sexual activity—nothing that could interfere with our intake, metabolism, and output of trace minerals and fats.

These rules are enjoined by the Department of Agriculture's HNRC, where human beings come to live for 2-9 months, and sign a contract to participate in experiments corroborating tests made on white rats and chickens. We signed a contract, yes, but it's as easily breakable as deciding to give in to craving, buy cigarettes or syrupy pancakes the next time out with the chaperon. Of what use then is the chaperon? Right. Not to physically stop us but to serve as a reminder, to be present should one of us suffer a sudden nicotine or sweets attack, and to supply understanding and patience.

Lord, I want a cigarette, then coffee, M&Ms, anything! So I force myself to think of this opportunity at HNRC, a time of *free* time. Eight of us have volunteered, although, for physical or psychological reasons, 25-33% of us won't stay. Undiagnosed hypertension was discovered in one volunteer the first week; another left after six weeks. Psychological screening forms the main basis for choosing volunteers; says Yvonne, a registered nurse (RN), "…some have different expectations of living in a controlled environment, so may get bored, depressed, homesick…" And as Eric, student volunteer and ex-Marine, puts it, "I feel a renewed appreciation of simple things…solitude, personal choices and opportunities…the lost opportunities…"

The staff tries to avoid those problems. The Minnesota Multiphasic Inventory (MMPI) test is used (566 always/sometimes/never-questions, like *I loved my mother* or *I never get depressed.*) Of hundreds of respondents to nationwide newspaper advertising they try to select the most suitable by asking often, "Can you keep yourself busy?" Most can. We read, take classes at the next door University of North Dakota (UND), shoot pool, go to the mall with the chaperon, get—in 1980 $20.00/day—and, in return, supply cooperation and will power, sometimes a minute-by-minute battle to stay and not quit.

I push away from my fold-down desk and walk four feet to the window and gaze at that cottonwood's clattery August foliage, some leaves already are showing the burnt-orange change to Autumn. As I stand there, the cravings for a smoke begin humming and buzzing through my whole being, producing a strange, sugary-like high, a floating sensation of wanting, *something*! God, how I want to taste nicotine, maple syrup, chocolate!—yes, sometimes chocolate craving is the strongest.

After almost six months without a cigarette I *do* quit, for two whole years. I won't stay quit until I start volunteering for drug studies (about 2001) at PRACs (now CETERO RESEARCH) in Fargo, North Dakota. Over my lifetime I have probably quit smoking two hundred times. I have thrown my last pack out of a moving vehicle, and then, the next day, went back and found them. Other times I've driven thirty miles round trip just to buy some. People trying to quit know what I'm talking about. Two minutes is the shortest time I've quit, then two days, then two weeks, then two years after HNRC. But not until PRACs did I quit for good. Strangely enough, it was easy cold turkey. But even after ten years I still want a smoke. Smoking to me was never a habit (something to do with my fingers…whatever.) No, smoking to me was a pleasure, something I did after accomplishing something, it was a reward, and, yes, sometimes the reward was as simple as finishing a meal. I started out on OASIS, but soon switched to straight CAMELS, then, after I restarted after HNRC, I went to MARLBOROUGH LIGHTS, but soon was breaking off the filter and lighting the filter end. Then after a few puffs I would put it out and smoke it again later, sometimes three and four times, and when I was broke I would save all the butts and roll them together, then I even started rolling the butts from butts, but that got to be a liiiiiittle too strong.

Now, when I want that reward I turn to a cup of coffee, and sometimes, just…nothing…. Yes, I still miss the good ole cigarette!

So I leave my room, walk down the sixty-foot hallway past the other volunteers' rooms, another forty feet through the exercise area, leap up two stair steps, push through a door and out onto a lower roof, our sundeck, an isolated place of sunshine.

The hot summer air hits my face. I breathe it, already easier for having not smoked, "You can't smoke here," Betty, RN, said during the initial phone contact. So, fine. I've wanted to quit but have lacked the will power. Several breaths later I'm relaxed and refreshed. The pounding pressure of right *now* selfish desire has passed again. I can face the rest of the day, the rest of the six months, maybe even the next meal.

Returning to my room I meet Donna, Head Nurse, a staunch authority figure whose order-keeping presence I appreciate. (She's never hard but we know she means what she says.) She gives me an understanding smile as if she knows, and I feel she *does* know. I feel all the nurses do know and understand.

****

Day Three of our 45% fat diet. Late September and nothing has changed except the oil. We switch from saturated coconut oil to polyunsaturated safflower. "We're trying to learn if absorption of iron is different depending on what type of fat," says Louise, dietitian-in-charge, "We think it is." Other trace elements tracked are copper and zinc. And like I said before, my experience was in 1980; the research they're doing there now is likely much different. My one gram of salt per day is rationed on quiche and tasteless reconstituted potatoes. Rationing makes me think about people in prisoner-of-war camps, truly harsh environments with many times fewer choices than this quasi-prison. I don't wonder for long. Such a comparison is embarrassing. I, at least, always retain the right to leave.

After about a half hour of resting and digestion the chaperon arrives to take us for errands. We enjoy that, not necessarily because it gets us out, but, also, into a van, way up above the rest of the traffic so we can see the rest of the world, a small, but pleasurably-anticipated thing.

In the beginning new volunteers go along mainly for the ride. Two have left; we've gained three. Dennis, Vietnam veteran and artist from California; Blaine, quiet rounder and aspiring writer from Iowa; and C. Victor, perceptive radical entrepreneur from many places. Soon, though, everyone is involved (classes, antique stores, bookstores.) Suddenly it's a race to get names listed on the bulletin board first. Nobody wants to wait or to keep anyone else waiting, and few want to share the chaperon, admirable people who get the brunt of our moods and tantrums.

At COLUMBIA MALL we pile out and soon pass THE CIRCUS, an electronic arcade. Some want to play so the others wait. Then a stroll past the fragrances of cookies, tobacco, ice cream —*CHOCOLATE*! Finally a destination: film. The moment the purchase is made, everyone, without a word, is ready to return to the lab.

While out in the normal world we look out for each other, and we've learned to respect each other's wishes pretty fairly, and we've even come to like each other; I even feel some lasting friendships have begun. But I think we've needed each other more, much, much, more, than we've wanted to be *with* each other. Too much of that time at the lab is too close, sometimes too tense, and, as time becomes more precious, woebegone to the volunteer who causes even a minor hardship to another volunteer. As Carl, coin collector and student volunteer from Wisconsin relates, sharing feelings of achievements and new friends, "...but I yearn for different companionship...never a break, always the same food, the same people..."

Day ends with a 9:45 p.m. snack. Bedtime at 11:30. I relax and sleep comes quickly.

****

I wake, and know it's soon time, although the October sky is still dark. 6:30 a.m. A knock. A few seconds pass, then the door cracks open. "Good morning, Jim," says Kay, exercise physiology technician. She pushes in the Metabolic Measurement Cart, which weekly gauges my basal metabolic rate. She smiles and hands me a nose clamp and mouthpiece. I place them while moving as little as possible. HNRC's interest now is to collect and analyze my expelled breath while at rest. Later it will analyze my breath as I ride the Ergocycle during prescribed exercise.

Kay reappears after ten minutes, "All done."

Sue, RN, the night nurse, comes in next to take my vital signs.

My favorite time of day is now. She smiles and hands me a thermometer, then sits on the edge of my bed and there is a sense of human contact. I see her through half-closed, still almost-sleeping eyes as she takes my blood pressure, pulse, respiration, and I accept the contact as comforting. On my part it's a subtle reception of strength to go on, to continue accepting this almost-no-privacy, very controlled life as *my* life, temporarily, and taking the scientific study of my metabolism—the daily/weekly, physical/psychological tests: metabolic rate at rest and during exercising, electrocardiograms, electroencephalograms, sweat collections, a glucose tolerance test, blood draws, underwater weighing, body scanning, muscle measurement, taste and olfactory tests, and others.

Wakeup is over. She's removing the thermometer, rising, leaving, gone. My duty now is to rise, slip on sandals and cutoffs, go to the bathroom and drain my bladder. Urine is collected in day-sized plastic bottles, stools in plastic bags… dehydrated and turned to powder before any researcher actually gets close to it, but, still, my name is on the bag. When business is finished in the bathroom one expects to flip that shiny little chrome handle and everything unpleasant is conveniently flushed away, gone from sight forever. But here at HNRC it becomes recorded research. Forever. And I can't just forget about it. Because I know somebody I know, or at least occasionally meet in the hallways, is making early-morning rounds collecting those frozen, *labeled*, bags of excrement.

They're also collecting jugs of urine, but that doesn't bother me nearly as much.

And food. That is measured to the hundredth of a gram. At meals we must eat every drop, every morsel, and then we must clean the dishes and utensils with our distilled drinking water, and then lick off the bowls and silverware, and then the kitchen workers inspect our dishes. To be certain we've done a good job.

After Wakeup I meet Sue in the exercise room for my weight. "48.8 kilos," She says, "Three days in a row." Thank God, I think. My weight runs in cycles but my reprieve is good for another three days. They won't raise my calorie level and I won't have to stomach anymore of that food.

Sue calls my weight to Hank, research physiologist and Bill, exercise physiology technician, and then is gone until tomorrow. I step down from the scales and approach my least favorite test of the week. Physical work capacity.

First a pre-exercise blood draw by Kay. Moments later I sit on the Ergocycle, waiting during a five-minute pre-exercise rest-period. Three EKG electrodes cling to my chest, a screw-down clamp closes my nose, a plastic tube in my mouth leads to the Metabolic Measurement Cart.

"Begin on the top of the minute, Jim." Bill says.

My attention goes to the timer. I have twenty seconds to prepare my mind, if not my body, for the task. Ten seconds. Hank snaps on the Metronome—*five*—causing a pervasive clicking and a blinking light I must get into rhythm with. *ZERO.* My legs begin pumping. I watch the EKG digitals of my heart rate move quickly from a restful 60 to 85-90, and then settle out.

After six minutes Bill increases the resistance to my peddling. My legs and mind push to the new assignment. My heart rate climbs to 110. I feel pressure in my arms and head but barely a beading of sweat.

Six minutes later he increases it again. A lot. My heart rate zooms to 130 and more. I see Kay placing a chair nearby. One minute to go.

"Stop on zero, Jim" Bill says. Fifteen seconds remaining.

Ten. Five. Three—"Stop."

As if he had to tell me.

All three, hanging onto electrodes and breathing tube, and *me*, assist me in getting to the chair, where Kay must do a post-exercise blood-draw within one minute before my heart rate slows too much and blood acidity changes. Puffing, not really caring about anything except resting, I stretch my arm to her. She takes charge now, gently, skillfully balancing my limp arm on her leg and introducing the needle. The post-draw is not always easy, but, seconds later it's all over. I'm free to sit and relax and watch as my heart rate returns to normal. This was the exhaustion session; most sessions are not so tough.

****

Early breakfast for three of us, then to old St. Michael's Hospital for underwater weighing. Eric goes first. I'm second so I change into cutoffs and sandals, get a dry weight, then a hot shower. Finished I join Mark, flutist and student volunteer from southern Minnesota. For ten minutes we philosophize on bagpipes, Italian history, our past Navy days, and the cute young ladies on UND campus.

My turn comes in the four-by-seven-foot, waist-deep tank. It's not my favorite test but I enjoy the warm water. The part I mind is exhalation underwater, as Hank says, I'm, "...one of our variables..." The exhalation reduces the volume of gas in the lungs which must be determined and subtracted from the apparent body volume. Hank knew after my first weighing, "Smoker, huh?"

Yes, but ex. The nicotine attacks have decreased during the weeks becoming months. The only thing remaining is the desire, the insidious fact that I've enjoyed smoking.

****

By Friday most tests have been done. But slow days bring extra boredom, frustration if minor things don't go right, anger and sarcasm at the slightest provocation. No matter how many ways a volunteer may claim he can entertain himself, or how much he says the tests cut into and ruin his day, too much free time under guard, and self-denial of life-pleasures, can bring about the boiling points.

Noon. A barely off-color joke is told by volunteer #1. A barely discernible sneer issues from volunteer #2. Then a very off-color joke comes from #3, which brings a direct request from #2, "Not at the table, please." Which brings a violent, pent up snarl back from #3, causing #4 to interrupt supporting #2's rights, finally causing #5 to interfere supporting #3 and suggesting #2 and #3 should be allowed to hash it out uninterrupted, which ends it, bringing painful, ear-shattering silence for the remainder of the meal.

In the afternoon an announcement appears on the blackboard for a special meeting with the staff psychologist, which brings talk and smoke screens from both sides. From John, born-again Christian jogger studying for the ministry, he calls our situation, "...negative, dangerous..." Does this young man have experience of what can happen among men confined, even loosely as we are? A good suggestion finally is offered: Meetings.

So maybe regular meetings to facilitate communication will be a contribution from this group of volunteers, or maybe a recreation director. Added expenses, yes, maybe, but more expensive should a volunteer quit in the middle of a study period.

****

Saturday morning brings Whole Body Count. I shower special, don a green scrub suit, eat breakfast, then later descend one story to a massive room within a room, with walls of steel almost six inches thick from pre-World War II ships (before radioactivity in the air.) I am trusted that far unchaperoned. No pop or candy machine lurks in the stairwell. No matter how trustworthy a volunteer may appear to be he still can't be trusted: Should he take even one bite of a food foreign to the study or one drink from a public water fountain, even by accident, it could mean ruination of that particular study.

I remove my sandals and lie down on a hard table, my face just inches below a 12-inch diameter disc housing a four-inches-thick sodium iodide crystal (another one below the table) that senses radioactivity from my body, then locates, identifies, and passes signals to the computers.

The 12-inches-thick door clunks closed, the room darkens,

music begins, and I look up at the disc and remind myself that it's counting, not zapping. Eventually we all get one radioactive meal (with wheat intrinsically labeled by stem injection with Fe-59.) Fourteen minutes pass. Whole Body Count is the last weekly test.

****

Sunday brings relaxation. Even though not a job and little responsibility, I still wait for Sunday, and possibly a trip to TURTLE RIVER STATE PARK (silence, mystery, solitude.) Especially this week because one of the shorter-termed volunteers leaves tomorrow, meaning five of the months have passed! One to go. The rest of us are now all short-timers!

****

Snow is piled a foot up my window. The cottonwood beyond is gray bare against a pale November sky. We'll spend Thanksgiving here and get the same food as every other day. And it's shocking to realize we've lived here such a long time.

Silver-gilded for me because I've done much reading and studied many things, and I've quit smoking, and I feel guilty thinking back to silly and immature arguments with the other volunteers, and of gagging over perfectly palatable meals, and of impatience with chaperones, dietitians, nurses who couldn't give me my wishes instantly, and of the loneliness…the reluctance to establish any sort of relationship in the outside world—and I continue comparing this seemingly-easy ordeal with what others have gone through, especially prisoners-of-war. They went through so much worse but had no choice but to stay, do their best, pull together and plot against their enemies, their guards, but here the guards do not hold guns. Our guards are friendly and kind and do not force us to stay.

Here our only real guards have been our consciences, our will power, ourselves, and in spite of ourselves, I, and the others, have learned about people, and life, and have grown.

We leave a little before Christmas. My dad and my nephew, Larry, arrive to take me home. I sit next to the window and look out as HNRC and many memories fade…and a few scalding tears do escape.

16

SYDNEY

We're on our way to Sydney, New South Wales, Australia. We'll spend two weeks there for Christmas, 1965. I have recently turned twenty-one and recently earned my first crow, a red chevron on my left arm. I am now a Torpoman's Mate Third Class Petty Officer, E-4. Yes, even with the flooding in the After Room fiasco. Later I would pass the test for E-5 but not high enough for advancement.

Australia, of course, is south of the equator. Which means, again, that we have to stop and us shellbacks have to initiate those pollywogs. But Archerfish has a more experienced crew. There aren't as many nonqualified personnel, so, consequently, there also aren't so many pollywogs. Out comes the lengths of fire hose, the garbage chute tunnel, the royal baby, King Neptune and his queen, and out comes the pirate costumes. Even I dressed up, but instead of a length of fire hose I wielded a camera.

We carry out the ceremony, eat hardily, splice the main brace (a shot of whiskey), fire the small arms, swim in the ocean (again, I didn't; that water is just too dang deep for me), and then get back underway for Sydney.

I do a little drinking, tourist exploring, and there I meet Sue, hair black as the night, luscious blue eyes, and skin with the softness and luster of new fallen snow. The absolute love of my life. But we didn't get together right away.

On the very first night, my good friend Everett Wenke has two girls. Sue is one. He asks me to entertain the *other* one. (God, I don't even remember the *other* one's name!) But, I agree. We explore Sydney, eat, and try the rides at the amusement park. At the end I take my girl home, meet her parents, and then spend the night making out with her. She isn't who I want to be with, though, but she *is* there, so, but, anyway, we don't go all the way and I go back to my boat the next morning with the worst case of lover's nuts I ever hope to have. Ever!

I spend the next days basically just being there, wasting our Christmas leave. I don't have much fun. My good buddy Everett, it turns out has a girlfriend at home who he plans to marry, so he turns Sue loose and suggests I take her out. A good idea, but, I have already latched onto this idea that one does not have sex with the nice girls (my buddy didn't have sex with her either) so, I don't call her.

So she calls me.

I'm in the Control Room, probably feeling sorry for myself, when the call comes. It's for me. I can't believe it.

For a bit I don't know who is calling. She's about to hang up when I come to my senses. Yes! YES! I remember, and I agree to see her.

So she comes down to the pier where we're moored, and then we go off on the adventure of discovering each other. I remember especially that crowded little ferry boat ride across Sydney harbor. I don't remember where we were going. Maybe just riding. But I remember the ride.

We're beside each other. The little ferry boat is tossing and turning gently. I have my left arm around her bare shoulders. She lays her head back. She looks at me, her eyes closing partway. The world becomes hazy and reduces to just the space left between us. The boat is crowded but nobody is too close. We could as well be alone. I lean toward her. She's relaxed, and trusts me, and doesn't pull away. I lean closer. My right hand moves to her face. Her eyes close, and mine close as our lips come together.

And talk about rockets and collision alarms.

Her soft lips become food for my soul. Her taste, her touch, her manner becomes unending memory. What is it about that one woman who can stir a young man's genes and hormones? This is my first romantic kiss as an adult. The image and wonder of it has stayed with me for forty-three years. Sue, I will never forget you.

17

THE BOTTOM

From that, to this. And what a title for a chapter.

I don't know if everybody reaches a point in their life when they feel they just cannot go on, but I did. It probably started in my early twenties, after that first farm auction, and the beginning of a back problem (just days after my discharge). I don't remember being depressed but I definitely remember losing direction. I had just spent four years and three months in the Navy having fun and adventure, yet anticipating returning to the farm. But the back problem, which evolved to a slipped disc, arthritis, and hospitalization, suggested otherwise, that I could never be a farmer. Everybody said so. I was just a twenty-two-year-old kid, so what did I know? So I believed the adults. So I had to make a life change.

So began those six months of higher education, and that long string of jobs. Then came a return to the farm after the first auction, but I kept my town job too. I should mention here that I never got help for my back or the arthritis, not that I didn't try. But no doctor helped and no medicine or therapy helped, but I was going downhill fast, so I started doing my own research. In the sixties we didn't have the internet, so I had to use books (I love books!)(I always have!)

I don't mean to start preaching here but I found out that the health of your body, depends a whole lot on what you put into it. (Imagine that!) From the beginning of my life I had paid no attention to diet and nutrition. But, from my reading I knew I had to go on a crash diet. So I did. I stopped meat, candy, pop, white sugar, white bread, went to whole wheat bread and skim milk, and as much fresh fruit and veggie as I could stomach, etc., etc. This diet was hard core for at least two years; since then I have moderated. No, I didn't eliminate arthritis but I did stop its pain and spread. And the physical back problem I learned how to give myself treatments and have not been back to any doctor for either reason for thirty-five years. No, I won't describe what helped my back. In order to do it, one must first be slim and flexible and, more importantly, believe in what you're doing. Most important: Do your own research. Don't depend on somebody else to tell you.

Getting back to my story, I, at first, thought I shouldn't get too detailed. I've changed my mind. I'm telling all. It's not going to be easy. So leading up to that bottom were the two farm auctions, two failed businesses, two failed love affairs, etc.

And there were other failures, just minor ones but each one sunk another nail. My mid-to-late-twenties became a very dark period in my life. I voluntarily put myself in the state mental hospital at Jamestown, North Dakota, and then twice voluntarily entered the veterans' mental hospital at St. Cloud, Minnesota, and there were others, too foggy to even remember. Each time I signed myself in and signed myself out. My depression was never a chemical imbalance, and prescription drugs did nothing but cause me to be tired and lethargic. Never high.

There were many thoughts and plans on how to *do it*, before the very bottom. Twice—*twice*!—I bought a handgun. Both times I parked somewhere in the forest in Minnesota. Yes, once I actually put the barrel in my mouth. No, I didn't cock it. Why not? Because I might have slipped, or I might have changed my mind as I was pulling the trigger, and caused not death but a horrible wound instead.

Another time I found what looked like a perfect dead end. A

huge concrete abutment supporting a railroad. The ditch was only slightly slanted, almost flat. It looked like it would be easy to hit it full speed, but, again, what if I changed my mind at the last second? Again, likely, horrible, horrible, wounds.

But no matter what I thought, or imagined, or planned, nothing changed. I had no plans for any kind of future; I just wanted things to end. Finally, I did reach the bottom. No specific reason, just the bottom. You fill a pail with water and eventually it gets full, and then runs over. That's what happened with me. I simply got full. I don't remember what year it was or my age, I just reached the bottom…and began to—absolutely this time—premeditate a murder:

Mine.

****

I had a traveling sales commission job. I hated it but it was providing living money. At the time I had an apartment, so I was nowhere near my parents or any member of my family. I was as alone as possible.

I made an appointment to see a doctor and complained, about being unable to sleep. A lie. I can still see him sitting there at his desk. I don't think he suspected the direction I was heading, but I remember what he said: "You should try talking to somebody sometime." Well, maybe he did kind of suspect.

Anyway, I shook my head and agreed. Another lie: I *didn't* agree. In the end he gave me a prescription for Darvon sleeping pills.

I had already heard, *somewhere*, that Darvon would do the job, but I didn't know if the amount I had would be enough, so, now get this, I didn't even open that bottle. I waited, continuing my job and my life, until enough time went by for that amount of pills to be gone, then I got the prescription refilled. Whether the pharmacist had to call the doctor for permission I don't know. Then I had my second bottle. I was pretty sure now that I had a lethal amount.

Suicide by sleeping pills. What a weenie-ass way to end it, but, I was ready. But I couldn't do it in my apartment. Because I was alone I knew it would be some time before I was even missed, by anyone. I didn't want to stink up the whole building, right?

So, I rent a motel room. In the room I waste no time and start pouring those pills down like there's no tomorrow, and, for me, in my mind right then, there wasn't going to be another tomorrow. When both bottles were empty I didn't even take my coat off but just lay down on the bed to wait....

How long I laid there I don't know. But, suddenly, just out of the blue, like a light bulb clicking on, I changed my mind. I didn't think about how hurt my parents would be if I did this, I didn't think of any other person. I just simply changed my mind about dying—I became *afraid* to die. I didn't know what would come next and I didn't want to find out like this.

I left the bed and went to the desk clerk and told him what I had done.

I don't remember him, I don't know what he did, but shortly the police and an ambulance were there. I remember sitting and riding in the back. Then I remember walking into the emergency room and seeing nurses and other people dressed in white hurrying toward me, but I am embarrassed at causing all this fuss, so I wave my hand and say; "Don't worry, I'm all right!" or something to that effect.

I remember seeing them stop, sliding even, as if they had put on brakes. I must have convinced them, and I must be thinking that what I actually took was a bottle of M&Ms. The next thing I remember is sitting down on something low to the floor. During those passing seconds, or minutes, in my rapidly disappearing awareness, I must have convinced myself, too, that everything was all right. I remember those people in white going about their business, and nobody was near me. I must *really* have convinced them...I, *kind of,* remember tipping over. I think I tipped to my left....

****

The next thing I remember is waking up in the hospital room. My parents are there and my sisters, Helen and Gerry, and my brother-in-law, Don. I remember all their faces. I'm sorry, my loved ones, I didn't mean to cause you this trouble. And there's an absolutely uncomfortable breathing tube in my throat. I can't talk. It's just as well. And my chest hurts, a lot.

Later I will hear that a doctor hit the center of my chest with his fist to restart my heart. That's how close I came to finding out what's waiting on The Other

Side after committing murder. Probably not a lot of forgiveness, at least not for murder by suicide. Probably just a quick return trip through that tunnel with the bright light at the end and right back out into the cold world as a squalling infant, with no—almost no—recollection of your past lives to help you do right in this one. Just an occasional strange déjà vu feeling. Not much. (God, I hope reincarnation isn't true!) And if it is true, do we have to keep coming back and coming back until we get it right? What if we never get it right? What then? Actually I wouldn't mind living my life over, that is, *my* life (but only if I could remember all I've learned in this life) and not have to start all over again with a whole new identity.

****

This wasn't easy to write, folks. It's embarrassing to admit to being so weak. My parents are gone, so they won't have to read this. My sisters probably will, though, and nieces and nephews. And some of my friends will. I hope nobody will think any less of me. And I'm not just clearing my head. I know people commit suicide all the time, I don't know how many, but I know they do. Maybe someone who reads this will be considering suicide, and then will see how close I came, and how dangerous it is to fuck around with one's life.

No, I didn't re-enter a mental institution because I knew there would be no help there…for me. For some, yes, there is help. I did go to therapy for awhile, even group therapy, but I finally came to realize that only one person in the world is responsible for me, and for my happiness, and that is me. And *only* me.

When my parents and Julia died, that was a hard time for me. Yes, I spent two years *not* depressed, exactly, but not exactly happy either, but I came out of it, and made the decision to leave town and move back to the country. That is nine years ago and I've never looked back.

Which brings us to my last chapter and that **banging** door.

18

HOME AGAIN

Home again. What exactly does that mean? No, I didn't get to return to the original storybook farm. I bought a piece of pastureland exactly two and one half miles straight west of it. The 1955 tornado probably began right in this exact spot, because there was a hole torn in the original highway, and that is just about one hundred feet from my house. Sometimes that speculation bothers me, but maybe a tornado is like lightening and never strikes in the same spot twice. Or so they say....

OK, you read the first chapter awhile back, so I'll go back a ways to remind you. The wind (gusts to 50mph) had just blown my newly-installed second-hand door against the house and woke me up, and my belongings were literally blowing away. Originally I had piled everything on the slab north of the house. I should have remembered that most strong wind in this country comes from the northwest, but I didn't. So, I began the task of moving everything from the north slab to the south slab and again piling everything on pallets, covering with a tarp, tying it down, and holding the tarp down with 35-pound concrete blocks. A tarp will do a lot if one can hold it down, but if the wind gets under the tarp that thirty-five-pound block could as well be made of Styrofoam—as I found out more than once. Many of my belongings would stay outside under that tarp in the snow and wind and rain for over two years, and before that, big items like the couch, wood stove, filing cabinets, etc., would lay out in the pasture on covered pallets for over two and one half months. For awhile I sometimes felt somewhat emasculated.

Anyway, I work for twenty-four hours in that wind, even after I'm exhausted. I had no choice but to keep going, because the wind kept going. And it could have rained. It didn't but it could have.

Before I go on I want to thank some people, but, I have to backtrack a bit. After the second farm auction the land was sold as well. This time there would be no going back. My parents retired to Abercrombie, North Dakota, and I eventually, joined them and bought the house next door. A whole nuther long string of jobs happened but I won't touch on them, just the main one, and I'll skip to that last year: 1999.

I made some good friends in Abercrombie, including Denny Herrick, a good drinking buddy (back in the day, that is) and who I went on a three-day canoe trip with, most of it spent in rain. Denny helped immensely with my move. I remember when we hauled out a load of firewood in his pickup. We were a bit top-heavy and about to tip over on my newly-selected road site, when I seriously/foolishly asked "Think I can get a cement truck in here?" He still chuckles about that.

Then there's John Larson, another good drinking buddy (also back in the day) and his wife Connie, who quite often invite me for a meal. And when I have a question about construction I ask John.

Others include Karl Snyder and Wendell and Joyce Odegaard (both Karl and Wendell helped me immensely when I was disassembling my greenhouse and then Karl transported all that lumber out to my new place.) Larry Syvertsen, who I worked with and who also helped with my move. Larry Slinger (who helped me prepare for the auction sale and my move) and his mother. Clayton and Joan Lee, who helped me more times than I have space for here. And there are others....

And Marlowe and Belva Haverland, whose tree removal and stump grinding service I worked for. That was my second favorite job of all time, Marlowe, thanks, man! (My first favorite was test-driving new cars of the CHRYSLER brand through the cold freezing streets of Fargo for two winters.) Anyway, I spent many good times working for, and with, Marlowe. He was my employer and also my friend, and he saved my life once. It was my last night of serious drinking, even worse than drinking my dolphins. Marlowe checked on me the next morning. I thought I was dead and was desperate for a can of COCA COLA, the only true cure for a sick hangover that I ever found. Marlowe went back up town and got me a COKE, thereby saving my life. Thanks, my friend Marlowe.

Moving on, some of those same guys helped put up my four walls and roof that day, which would also include Rick Fowler, Johnny Olson, John Wesolowskie, and Curt Vangsness. When I finally got settled in for the winter I sent out thirty-five thank-you cards, and I hope I included everybody.

A second day, my good friend, Rick Fowler—and his wife Debbie, who brought sandwiches—came again and directed operations, and my family came, my sister, Gerry, brother-in-law, Don, and all four of their sons, my nephews, Michael, Larry and Robert, even Kevin and Kathy, from Minneapolis, MN. We shingled, closed up the ends, put in a door and two windows. What a great day with my family!

This maybe would be a good time to give some room to my whole family, because, without that group of loving people who knows where I'd be or what I'd be...probably alone on a street somewhere, not even knowing who I am. I've tried to say something good about each member, and that has worked pretty well until I got to my nieces and nephews by marriage, and that's only because I haven't spent the same *kind* of time with them. They are all special and important to me too, so I asked this question of them: What, besides your family and job is important to you? Not everybody got back to me but I know some stuff about most of them anyway. The list that follows is going to remind you of chapters 35 and 36 (maybe more) in the book of GENESIS.

After the tornado, Helen and Clayton were blessed with three more daughters, Mari, Peggy and Patti, before Clayton was killed in an automobile accident in 1976. (I thought the world of Clayton; he was always kind to me and encouraged me in whatever endeavors I took on; he also was in the Navy toward the end of WW II. He took me fishing, often helped with our farm-work and eventually became an auctioneer.) Helen went on and Married Duane a few years later, and we all got blessed with her two new stepchildren, Bruce and Angie. Today Helen does craftwork and loves her grandchildren and pets: Lucy the dog and Tiger and Sassy the cats. I've come to know and think the world of Duane too; he's a blacksmith who can manufacture just about anything, and, even though partially crippled, he has a full schedule with high school students and adults in his Welding Technology School.

Curtis, Helen's first-born, grew up to join the National Guard, become a construction contractor, then a long-haul truck driver, married Bev, and they are blessed with Sandy and Curtis junior. From Sandy, my first great-niece, I got Hannah, my first great-great niece, and Hannah is far into high school already, so, someday she might just make me a great-great-great uncle—and, sorry, but that's the only great-great one I'll mention.

Mari married Russ and produced Mark, Marisa, Carrie and Ryan; Mari also got a stepson, Jason, who I haven't even met. (See how extended a family can get?) Mari is the only newborn baby I can remember coming home from the hospital. I remember gazing at that beautiful golden baby in a white bassinet, and she has kept that special and mischievous beauty right into adulthood. Mari also loves her husband, four children and four grandchildren, and loves to cook with a girlfriend at the Elk's Club, and just being outside while hunting in Montana in the fall. Maybe I remember Mari so clearly because she was the first new baby after The Storm. Mari's husband Russ also took me to Minneapolis to see the Twins play Seattle. I believe the Twins won that day.

Peggy arrived next, a brunette, also a beauty, and a charmer; she could have been a model, but chose instead to marry Ben and produce Brady and Bryan. Peggy has a great laugh and loves horses and feels lucky to have found peace and contentment in life. Her two grown boys—as they continue to grow—she hopes will find the same.

Patti, another golden blonde, is the baby of the family (like me) and is still one of the cutest, and she's the one who gave me that special hug on my first or second Navy leave. One of her favorite places is that cowboy capital of North Dakota, Medora. She also produced our Lee Ann.

I don't see much of Bruce and Angie, but I do know that Bruce drives a race car and Angie has a new baby and a job in the defense department and married Curt, who is manager of a chain of restaurants.

Gerry went to NDSSS, Wahpeton, ND, later started work with the county government, and married Don, and they are blessed with Debbie, Michael, Larry, Robert, and Kevin. Gerry is our traditionalist, keeping alive the important parts of the many holidays. At Gerry's wedding I was gift taker with Wanda, Don's really cute cousin. I always enjoyed having Don help us on the farm, hauling bales and milking cows. And it wasn't the work he saved us; I just plain liked having Don around. Don also taught me how to drive on our 40-acre hay meadow, and took me to many movies (one was FOR WHOM THE BELL TOLLS, with the late GARY COOPER.)

Debbie went to Moorhead State University (MSU), became an accountant, married Gene and they are blessed with Rayna, Lance and Megan; Debbie also got a stepson, Brady. She remembers and still cherishes her lifelong best friend, Marilee, from the first grade. What I'm going to say about Debbie might get me in trouble with my other nieces and nephews, but, this is supposed to be a *tell-all* autobiography. Right? Right. *Nearly* from the time Debbie came home from the hospital she was out-of-this world cute. I say *nearly* because I don't care what anybody says, I think all newborns not only all look alike, but they are not cute!

I suppose if I ever was a father I might change my tune.

Michael, also MSU, also became an accountant, married Sherry, and they are blessed with Caitlin and Josh. Mike shared that whenever he hears a mourning dove he feels homesick for his grandpa and grandma and that storybook farm I've mentioned. He also enjoys hiking in Glacier National Park and seeing the stars there at night—Oh, yeah, and playing cards and 70's & 80's Classic Rock Music. Sherry went to MSU and became an Analyst Programmer at Meritcare. She also enjoys hiking and sitting by a campfire, sunrises and sunsets, scrapbooking, blooming flowers, snowflakes and eating smores.

Larry, MSU, became a Service Coordinator in social work, married Shelly, NDSSS, and they are blessed with Amy. Before that, Larry followed his uncle into the Navy and became a Second Class Petty Officer, MS, E-5. He chauffeured and sometimes cooked for Rear Admiral Rogers. He and I have never discussed his adventures but I'm sure he had many. Besides that Larry likes throwing darts, playing softball with his brother Bob, fishing at Pleasant Lake, and watching the Minnesota Twins. Shelly is a Transcription Manager at Meritcare, and, according to Larry, could live in a mall and shop all day; she also collects CREATIVE MEMORIES pictures and spends two and a half days—yearly—at a camp with her sisters-in-law, Shelly and Brenda, scrapbooking and visiting.

Robert, NDSU, an advocate for the little people (not necessarily meaning children but the "less pretty" people of the world), became an industrial engineering specialist, married Brenda, and they are blessed with Nate and Luke (who very often reminds me of DENNIS THE MENACE cartoons.) Brenda, NDSSS, works at MERITCARE as a quality analyst, also is an Emergency Medical Technician (EMT), and volunteers with emergency responders, as EMT and sometimes ambulance driver. Robert says Brenda lives for that volunteer work. Bob himself lives for his sons and sports, and was thrilled this year (2009) when his alma mater, the NDSU BISON basketball team, went to the nationals for the BIG DANCE. (*I* even paid a little attention to that event.)

Kevin, MSU, became a computer programmer, married Kathy, and got two lovely grown stepdaughters, Sarah and Kim. I've never met those girls but I *have* seen their pictures. Kevin and Kathy really like just being together and doing things together, and hanging out with Sarah and Kim. For instance: There are 68 state parks in Minnesota, where they live. They have made it a quest to visit them all— not to just drive by—but to either hike or snowshoe in them, and they have already been to all but five.

I had a brother, Roger, who would have been older than me, but he didn't live very long. But I do have two older brothers, Don and Duane, my brothers-in-law.

Wow, that might not be as long as the list of names in the first book of the Old Testament Bible, but you can see where this is going. Sorry to all of you greats and great-greats that didn't get much mention. There is simply no end to you....

****

The first winter goes pretty well. I had enough wood from the year before to keep me warm, and, after all, I'm heating only sixteen by twenty-four feet, and my belongings are piled to the ceiling, so there isn't a lot of space left to heat. After an auction sale and getting rid of tons of stuff, I still have, tons of stuff. I didn't get a well dug, though, because that will cost thousands of dollars. Nine years later I'm still hauling drinking water and taking sponge baths with rainwater and melted snow.

I bought a compostable toilet (SUNMAR) and it's still working fine. I even fed the birds the first winter. Chickadees, nuthatches, woodpeckers, and a bunch of goldfinches.

Before I go further I must say that my first two years here were magic. I will share some of that right now, because this is the last chapter. For two years I am completely alone. My nearest neighbor east, across a pasture is one mile, North, through thick forest, one mile, south many, many, pasture miles, and west there is pasture after pasture and then the Sheyenne National Grasslands.

That's changed now: East and South haven't changed; north and west has, but I've accepted it. To the north now are my good neighbors, Orrin and Marlys. They sold me this land and have helped me immensely to get established here, especially Orrin who I went to often for construction knowledge. Marlys photographed me for my blog and often invites me to meals, and "coffee". To the west now, right across the highway (but behind trees) is Joe and Heidi and their daughter Aubrie. When I was trying to lift 4'x8'x5/8" sheets of plywood up to the second story, for the floor, I could get them to the scaffolding but no further. I called Joe, he came right over and in minutes we had them all up! Also across the highway are Dennis and Linda; Dennis leveled out some fill on my driveway with his scraper and has pulled me out of deep snow. I'm fortunate to have all good neighbors.

For the fight I sometimes have had getting started here people have often said to me, "You must pray to God a lot." "No," I answer, "But I *thank* God a lot." Especially for those first two years, and I thank Him almost every day for some small or large accomplishment.

My very first night here, early September, 1999, I spend in my car. I'm thrilled to hear a great horned owl and later a chorus of yipping and yapping coyotes. The next morning I look over the land and make plans. The moment I saw the place I knew where the house would be: Just over the hill but slightly behind it and about 450 feet from the present highway. A string of cottonwoods are east, an oak forest is north, prairie is west, and south is more grass and a wetland that comes and goes. In 1999 and 2000 there were so many waterfowl I almost needed air traffic control. Then it goes dry for two years. This year, 2009, it covers about 200 acres.

The amount of birds and other wildlife here is amazing, and the first snowfall...I'm lucky. I'm outside when it begins with huge flakes that float and tumble in the nearly windless air. It's mid-afternoon and no sun anywhere. The snow comes thicker but still just floating and tumbling. It's like a Currier & Ives Christmas card. I could be totally alone in the world here. I *feel* alone. The snow comes thicker still and the flakes get smaller and a very slight breeze begins and soon the ground is white.

One other snow event is memorable. I was at the end of the mail line, so, for the first three years I had to pick up my mail one mile to the north, where my closest neighbor lived. Later, when I get a neighbor across the highway who's a little past me, then there's two of us and the mail will be allowed to come this far. Anyway, before that, in winter, going, I always walked through the forest, where I'm protected from the north wind, and coming back I walked on the highway with the wind to my back. On one of these occasions I am returning, it is snowing (heavy, fluffy, flakes, again, and no wind) and also a bit foggy. I hear a familiar sound, yet not...kind of an eerie sound, especially if you can't see the source. I stop. In seconds, from the west out of the white murk, ghostlike, appear about twenty white swans, only about fifty feet away and forty feet above the highway. They disappear quickly, as if they hadn't been there at all.

One cold winter day my birds are perching in nearby trees. None are at the feeder. After several moments of observation I determine why. A northern shrike has appeared at the feeder, but it doesn't eat seeds. It's considered a perching songbird but what it eats is smaller birds, and now it's waiting for some dumb little bird to get careless. In the next days some definitely do. There are two species of shrike; the northern has a very obviously large head. But, yes, occasionally it does take a small bird. This is nature at work, folks. Whether the same bird or not I don't know, but a shrike appears every year for the next three winters. On the third winter I find a pile of gray and white feathers on the ground near the feeder. So the shrike has fallen to an even larger predator. But I have no idea what.

Two more winters pass. I have learned a bit of the carpenter trade and add twenty feet to my house, doubling its size. Future planning for solar heat includes quarter-inch Plexiglas, slanted to 23 degrees, on the south end. Even now, when the sun shines, it gets comfortably warm in there, and now I have a place for bedding plants in the spring, so my garden also doubles in size.

I see in my journal an entry for June 21, 2002: This is the mother of all light shows. The lightening is nearly continuous and almost blinding, and every few seconds a bolt goes streaking horizontally and the crash of thunder is instantaneous and ferociously loud. I jump every time..., and, feel some fear. The television radar shows the red passing right over my head, and it is. The rain is pouring straight down, but no wind, thank the Lord, but the lightening and thunder is nothing if not spectacular.

The main event passes. The lightening, now distant, continues but without the frightening crashes. I don my raincoat and hood and go outside. The rain continues but gently. Everywhere it seems, at torso level, there are little sprites of light that float for a few seconds and a few feet and then disappear, and then reappear and disappear and reappear: Fireflies, competing with the waning lightening.

Something is taking my lettuce and cabbage plants. I suspect a woodchuck so I set a HAVAHART TRAP. The next morning no woodchuck but a skunk. I've always liked skunks but have never had to actually deal with one. It appears to be a young one (but I'm sure its sprayer works) and right now it's asleep. But it's soon awake and sees me. The tail comes up, but it keeps facing me, then stomps its feet and makes some sort of hissing sound. I back away and return with a piece of plywood, and talk soothingly to it. Once the plywood eliminates our eye contact it appears to settle down again. I get the trap door open and the skunk, nonchalantly but with its tail high, leaves, with no threats to me at all.

The next morning a raccoon is in the trap, and it is not friendly at all. It thrashes about in the trap and growls, quite menacingly. So, I release it too. It doesn't leave nonchalantly but as a streak of gray. I never catch a woodchuck but, shortly, the raiding does stop.

Another storm event happens August 31, 2002. I stand at the east porch door. The rain has turned everything clear-white and is coming down sideways. That's how hard the wind is blowing. The tall cottonwoods to the east are whipping and leaning ferociously, worse than I have ever seen them. I have my raincoat on and am ready to go to the shed by the garden for protection. At least it is over the hill, protected by trees to the north and west, and maybe even would afford *some* protection from a tornado. I have *heard* that a hill might cause a tornado to jump, slightly. But I don't go. I stand there on the porch transfixed, not exactly terrified—*exactly*—but… afraid. I hear a vicious sound of…wind?...that appears to be in the distance, north, where I can't see, and *that* sound is distinct from the sound of the whipping cottonwoods. Is it a tornado coming to get me, *again*, and maybe finish the job this time?

These storms continue to fascinate me. I would rather watch them in awe than cower in hiding. I cannot believe another tornado would ever try to get me. It would not be fair! I am a fool.

One more phenomenon: There was no electricity here when I

came. This land had been a pasture, so my first construction work requires a generator to run my tools. One night it is stolen. I have an idea who took it but no proof. Anyway, my point is, there were no highline poles. When electricity arrives (Yes, I did get it before winter that first year), suddenly there are three highline poles on my land. One afternoon, probably late September the year I was building the south addition, the roof is on, everything is sealed up, so, yeah, I decide to take a break out there in that bright light and warm sun.

Barn swallows have always been one of my favorite birds, but what is sitting on the wires among those three poles is unbelievable. They are almost bird-on-bird, there has to be over a thousand. Tree swallows and other swallow species are likely among the barn swallows. I'm not sure, but what a sight! When they occasionally leave the wires (sometimes all at once) the wires jump and shake, even the poles appear to sway. The birds swoop and dive over the nearby grassland (probably catching lunch) then they all land on the wires again. They stay a couple hours. I have seen flocks of birds before, but nothing like this swallow spectacular!

Three more winters pass. Now I'm thinking of adding twenty-four feet which will cover the north slab, I'm even considering two stories. About in September I start. Winter comes. I complete the first story. By the next winter I'm climbing around rafters in twenty below zero weather. It's so cold I have to go in every half hour or so to warm up by the wood stove, and take my electric tools in every night because, if they're cold, they make strange whining sounds when I start them. By March I'm nailing on the last of the shingles.

Three more winters have passed. I still can't use most of my house because it's not finished, not all heated, not a lot of things. I chose not to get a mortgage and am building my house, basically, one board at a time, as I can pay for them. It's taking some time, it's been a long road, sometimes it's unreal that I have been allowed to come here to live, and stay, but, again, I have never looked back.

Like the music group TRIUMPH says, FIGHT THE GOOD FIGHT.

--the end—

Here's the fiction I promised.

WAITING TO DIE

FOR A HUNDRED YEARS MANKIND HAS FEARED THE PANDEMIC,

AN EXTRAORDINARILY-MUTATED VIRUS, THAT VICIOUS CREATURE THAT CANNOT BE SEEN BY THE NAKED EYE.

"She's resting quietly," the kind-looking, white-haired lady said, "First door on your left."

Derek Whitfield nodded but didn't smile. He had not had a female patient yet, and did not look forward to this one with too much happiness. He stopped outside the hospice room and stared at the patient's name. Susannah Brite, just black letters scribbled on white cardboard and taped to the wall. The patients were no longer getting top notch care. Basic care, yes. Food. Water. Bathing… sometimes.

The care-giving lady who had answered his knock at this house seemed very nice, and probably was giving excellent care. Not the case with most of his patients, least not *excellent* care. There were just too many sick people, and the victims were the age-group who should have been providing the care. Twenties and thirties, nineteen being the youngest yet to die, thirty-nine the oldest, with the most by far being between the ages of twenty-five and thirty-five. People over forty—it was reasoned—had maybe experienced enough viruses in their lives that they simply had built up a natural immunity. At least it was hoped that reasoning was true, *and* that simple.

But even with the shortage of professionals there was one stage of the sickness that got the best of care: The end of life, which usually lasted just one day, sometimes only hours. The signal of the end was the beginning of a lowering blood-pressure and a slight rise in body temperature: Shallow respirations, officially. End-of-life care could be given by just about anyone, so the word went out for volunteers: Age fourteen and above, no particular qualifications. Medical establishments soon had a list—though not a large one—of local volunteers. So when shallow respirations began, volunteers were called in the order their names appeared on the lists.

Derek Whitfield, age sixty-four, twenty-five-year Army veteran, qualified. It took him a long time to volunteer, seven months into the world-wide outbreak, long after the experts had deemed the face masks useless. Most volunteers kept wearing them anyway, but Derek refused. He considered the masks an insult to the victims. "Just be there for their end…," he was told. Somehow that seemed… useless. What difference could it make? They were dying. Most, after their week or so of suffering, probably just wanted to get it over with. Derek's attitude wasn't great, but he did think that what he was doing was important. And he did think most of his patients appreciated his presence.

****

Susannah Brite would be his forty-second patient. He had requested only young men, and—until then—had gotten only young men. He had thought they would be easier. They weren't. Some went out like men of honor: Stoic and at attention. Most went out not quite like that. Some even went out crying. Dying was dying, and nobody actually knew what waited on The Other Side, if anything. Derek was pretty sure nothing but blackness waited, but of course he never suggested that to anyone. "Just hold their hand," he was also told, "Kiss their forehead, or their cheek, if you want, if you think *they* want," and, most importantly, "Have a soothing voice."

That all had seemed easy enough. He hoped this woman would be that easy, and just one more number to him.

He raised his hand to knock. Usually nobody answered. The patient was usually alone when he arrived. Quite often not even family was available. In the new millennium families often were separated by thousands of miles, and often even lived on different continents. Very likely, when some young person got sick they didn't even have time to get home. And as more and more people died the travel industry soon became…less then efficient.

But at least everybody usually got a private room. When the hospitals filled, and the patient was determined to have that specific killer virus, he or she was immediately shipped to a private home. Large homes, once housing mostly university students, were used first, but they soon filled too. So any private home and even business places came to be used, if the owner could guarantee even the minimum basic care.

Derek's eyes closed. He released a breath, his fists tightened. He had about reached his limit for this unhappy business, he wasn't sure he could even face this young woman. He didn't know why he had finally agreed to even *see* a woman. A twenty-nine-year-old woman who should be in the absolute prime of her life, but instead was dying of a disease that science had yet been unable to control. Except for pain. Painkillers still worked, and the victims nearly always died before their body built up a tolerance to the painkilling drug. Even though bedridden and very weak the victims spent their last days in somewhat a state of euphoria.

A good thing—if anything about the disease could be called good—there was no disfiguring at the end, no oozing of sores or bleeding like in the movies, just organ failure, of *all* the major organs. So once that started the end came quickly.

His hand still raised to knock, Derek pulled it back to his forehead and squeezed his temples, and let out another breath. It was the sort of uncontrollable shallow breathing that he had experienced so many times in his life, always just before some dangerous activity, like waiting his turn to parachute, or waiting for a deadly storm to run its course, or drawing that first bead on an approaching Vietcong, a man he was soon to kill, if the man didn't kill him first.

But approaching these sick people was not dangerous. Breathing should have been normal. Physically, of course, they couldn't hurt him, but they always tried to break his heart. None did, but they all tried.

Very gently, he knocked, and released yet another very shallow breath.

No answer. The door was already open about a foot. He pushed it open further and, with one step, crossed that gaping chasm. And saw her, and released one last breath.

Her eyes were closed. Her face was pale. He imagined her cheeks being usually rosy, blending with the tiny freckles gracing both sides of her face and disappearing into that rich-looking, dark auburn hair...that appeared to be freshly washed and curled. *She must be getting really good hospice care here.* At least three pillows propped her up. Hospital beds for everyone were out-of-the-question, but pillows were cheap.

He took three steps to her bedside. Her eyes opened. Her mouth opened, slightly. She licked her lips, once on the upper lip, once on the lower, but no words came. Her eyes closed again. "Susannah, I'm Derek." He waited, "I'm here to spend some time with you..., if you would like that...."

Her eyes opened again. Her left hand raised, slightly, "Yes, I would," she said. Derek barely heard but he knew what she had said. They all said the same thing, and *he* always said the same thing. He put his left hand under her left hand, and felt her grip him with a strength that surprised him. The strength though, was short-lived, but the grip itself remained. Without even thinking about it he lifted her hand and leaned down, and pressed her hand against his cheek.

For a few seconds she gripped his hand tighter again, "Thank you, Derek," and again closed her eyes.

Barely above a whisper but he heard and understood. He then lowered her hand and placed his other hand, too, over hers. And there he stood, feeling what strength she still had gripping his hand. And he felt embarrassed, and a little angry, *Why, God? Why are you taking this beautiful young woman, and all the others? Does Heaven have a shortage of young people, or something? Why, God?—for Christ's sake! Why?*

Then he felt surprised for talking to God. If he truly believed everything only turned black after death, why on earth would he talk to God, who he, evidently, didn't even believe in?

****

Time passed, at least an hour. The grip in Susannah's hand remained. Derek had not moved. He didn't want to disturb even the air around them; he didn't want to cause her even an imagined discomfort, and he liked looking at her face. A peaceful, gentle, face, at peace with the world. She was so lovely. She probably had been a model, or an exercise diva, maybe an actress, or maybe even a sultry, enchanting, spy. No, she had been none of those things. He imagined her being a minister in her short life, or maybe a school teacher of very young children, or a nurse. Yes, a nurse, a hospice-care nurse. She probably had spent her last healthy days doing exactly what he was doing: Caring for dying people.

He thought of the women he had known, made love with, and for one reason or another, rejected: No values, or morals. No financial sense. No good sex. Too clingy, too whiny, too this, too that. He had never found a woman good enough to climb the very high pedestal he had set out for her, so, consequently, he had spent his life mostly alone. He loved women though, just didn't necessarily want one full time.

Susannah, he felt, would have climbed that pedestal easily. Her grip said she would have. No problem…

Her grip increased, "Derek…."

"Yes, Susannah…?" He loved the sound of her name,

Susannah, it seemed to roll off his tongue smoothly, like a small, sparkling, waterfall.

"I'm…thirsty…."

"I'll get you some water." He let go of her hand with his right hand and started to pull away. She held on. He stopped. "Susannah, I can't reach the water. I have to let go of your hand for a few seconds…."

"I'm sorry," she whispered.

But still she didn't let go. Maybe she couldn't. He brought his right hand back to her hand, first gently squeezed her hand and patted it, then, one finger at a time, he loosened the hold she had on him. Instantly his hand felt cold and alone. That thought shocked him, that he was missing her touch, even *wanting* her touch.

He got the water from a nearby table. A glassful. Probably that was stupid. She maybe couldn't lift her head enough. Very likely she couldn't. There was something else where the water was. He returned. A white sock. It looked clean. He smelled it. It smelled clean. He returned to Susannah, dipped the sock in the water, then touched her lips with it, and gently squeezed it.

Her eyes stayed closed but her lips opened, "Ummmnn…." Her tongue moved against the sock. The sounds she made reminded him of times making love. The *good* times making love. The good women he had made good love with, and then aimed them toward that very high pedestal that none could climb, so he had rejected even the good ones…for one reason, or another. But he would never have rejected Susannah—

Footsteps. Loud footsteps in the hall, then at the door, "Sir?" An approach, and a slightly-muffled, not-nice-sounding voice, "I'm going to have to ask you to wrap this up."

Derek faced the speaker, faced the wide-open, wildly-staring eyes above the face mask, then returned the sock and water to the table, then returned to Susannah, put his hands on her shoulders, and squeezed them, "Sweetheart, I'll be right back." *Sweetheart*. How long since he had called anyone '*Sweetheart*'? Maybe a niece long ago, or maybe a young daughter of one of his girlfriends that he rejected…for one reason or another. Then he took the arm of the owner of the voice and escorted him quickly, and somewhat harshly, through the door and then away from the door, hopefully far enough to be out Susannah's hearing, "What the hell are you talking about? This woman can't be moved. She's dying!"

The eyes above the face mask got even wilder, "She's a fucking whore!"

Derek felt his mouth fall open, and for just one tenth of one second he felt dismay at the news, then felt anger at feeling that dismay.

"Yeah, right, they didn't tell you that, did they?"

"You son-of-a-bitch," Derek poked his right index finger into the man's chest, which made the man step back, "I don't care what she was in another life. Now she's waiting to die! She deserves the dignity of any other human being."

"Christ, she's been here over a week—she should've died by now!"

"You bastard." Derek spun the man, then escorted him to the door and through it, then grabbed him by the scruff of neck and seat of pants and pushed him off the porch onto the lawn.

The man landed and rolled, "Mutherfucker! You think you can just throw me out of my own house?"

"I just did."

"Well, I want that woman out of there. I need to get it cleaned up. I've got a new renter coming for Christ's sake!"

"Well, you'll have to go through me to do it, and I don't recommend you try."

"Mutherfucker, I'll be back with the police!"

"You do that."

****

Derek stepped back inside. The woman of the house, the very nice woman he had spoken with earlier, was there, "I apologize for my brother, sir, but he owns this house. I just care-take for him. He's been on me all week for even allowing this."

"You mean the girl...."

"Yes, but there are so many. I felt I just wanted to help."

"You did right ma'am." Derek turned to start toward Susannah's room, but then waited and faced the woman again.

"He *will* return with the police, sir." Her face was stonily sober.

"But surely the police will support Susannah's staying here."

"Maybe six months ago they would have." The woman's face remained sober, "But now there are so many sick...people are getting overwhelmed...and impatient."

"How about you?"

"Me? What?"

"Will *you* support her staying here?"

The woman's face changed. Still sober, but after a few seconds, "Yes. I will."

"Good." Derek nodded and started away again.

****

In Susannah's room Derek quickly got the sock and water and returned to Susannah's side, "I'm here again, Sweetheart." He dipped the sock and again placed it on her lips, and gently squeezed it.

She again made the appreciative sounds, and, this time, opened her eyes.

Those eyes. Derek felt sincere love for this woman enter him.

"I heard what that man said."

Her voice was little more than a whisper, but Derek had no trouble understanding her, "That man is a fool, Sweetheart."

"He said the truth."

Derek set the water and sock aside, then grasped both Susannah's hands, "Don't worry about what he said. I don't know what will happen, but I won't let them take you, and I won't leave you."

More time passed. A lot. Derek remained in the same position, but he was getting tired. He longed to sit down for just a few minutes.

The care-taking woman appeared at his side, "I know you haven't moved for at least two hours, sir. I'll hold her hand for awhile." She nodded toward a cushioned chair, "Go sit."

"I…." He didn't know what to say.

"Go ahead. I'll stay with her. Anyway, I've been giving her basic care all week."

"All right. Thank you." Derek sat, and felt every muscle and bone relax. He hadn't realized how tired he had become, but then for years, since leaving the army, he had done nothing to stress himself so. The hours spent with his other forty-one patients, all men, he had often sat down, but of course had never left the room except to relieve himself. The restroom usually was not far away. Here…, "Ma'am, may I use your bathroom?"

"It's upstairs."

He didn't know if he wanted to get that far from Susannah, but, he had to go. So he did, "I won't be long."

****

Only about three minutes had passed when Derek heard the scream, and his name called out. He zipped up and cleared the stairs in four leaps, and heard the care-taking woman trying to comfort Susannah as he reached the room's door, "…went to the bathroom."

He hurried to her bed and put his right arm above and around her head, and his left hand on her right cheek, and pressed his right cheek against her left cheek, "Sweetheart, I'm here. I *won't* leave you. I promise." He leaned back. There were tears in her eyes, "I won't leave you, Susannah. This kind lady was just giving me a break. You know her."

"I'm sorry." Susannah's eyes were open, "When I didn't see

you I became so afraid…that you had left me."

Derek moved his left hand back to her hand, "You sound stronger, Susannah." He stood up straight, "Are you getting better?"

"Yes. I think so."

"That's good." Derek moved back to his regular position and began holding both her hands again, and, from the corner of his eye he saw the care-taking lady shake her head, negatively. He glanced at her and nodded that he understood. Susannah was not getting better. Sometimes they appeared too. He knew that, but it was always only temporary, and usually happened just before the end. He wasn't ready for Susannah's end. He didn't *want* her to end, and he knew that when she did end it would hit him harder than his other forty-one patients all put together.

Time passed again. The care-taking lady had left and Susannah had long ago quieted, again, and, *weakened,* again...except for that grip in her left hand. It wasn't much, but definitely a grip, a sign that she still held onto life…and onto him. He gazed at her face. Angelic she was, so peaceful. When her time came, surely God would take her completely into His arms. Having experienced a woman like Susannah was changing Derek's mind about The Other Side. Surely there was more than darkness.

She stirred, "Derek…," her eyes opened, "Please don't hate me for what that man called me."

"I don't hate you, Sweetheart."

"But, don't you wonder, why, I did it?"

"Actually, Susannah," he smiled, the first since arriving, "No. I haven't been wondering why. You…probably didn't have a choice."

"But I did. I know some girls don't, and are abducted into prostitution, but I did have a choice. I was what they call…a high-end prostitute."

Derek didn't know what to say, so kept quiet.

Susannah was quiet too, for a moment, then went on, "I did it because it was good money. But for you, Derek, I would do it for free. But now I can't."

Again, Derek did not know what to say.

"Say you don't hate me, Derek."

"I don't hate you, Sweetheart." He smiled again, "I could never hate you."

"I love it when you call me 'Sweetheart.'" She choked, slightly, "Nobody ever has."

"Everybody else is a fool." Derek kept a hold on her hand and moved up to her head, leaned down, kissed her cheek right above her upper lip and next to her nose.

"Thank you, Derek. I love you." Then the grip in her hand at last relaxed. She was gone, but she had stayed as positive as could be expected to the end.

Derek whispered, "I love you, too, Susannah, my one true sweetheart."

****

When the house's owner, the police, and the medical authorities arrived, Derek Whitfield, the staunch twenty-five-year army veteran, his heart at last broken, still stood holding the lifeless hands of Susannah Brite. And he stayed with her right up until her cremation, then took home the ashes of his forty-second—and last—patient.

the end